WALLENBERG
THE MAN IN THE IRON WEB

ELENORE LESTER

Prentice-Hall, Inc., Englewood Cliffs, New Jersey 07632

ISBN 0-13-944322-3

ISBN 0-13-944240-5 {A REWARD BOOK : PBK.}

Wallenberg: The Man in the Iron Web
by Elenore Lester
© 1982 by Elenore Lester

Printed in the United States of America
Prentice-Hall International, Inc., London
Prentice-Hall of Australia, Pty. Ltd., Sydney
Prentice-Hall Canada, Inc., Toronto
Prentice-Hall of India Private Ltd., New Delhi
Prentice-Hall of Japan, Inc., Tokyo
Prentice-Hall of Southeast Asia Pte Ltd., Singapore
Whitehall Books Limited, Wellington, New Zealand

10 9 8 7 6 5 4 3 2 1

Library of Congress Cataloging in Publication Data
Lester, Elenore (date)
    Wallenberg, the man in the iron web.

    Bibliography: p.
    Includes index.
    1. Wallenberg, Raoul.   2. World War, 1939–1945 –
Civilian relief–Hungary.   3. Jews—Hungary—History—
20th century.   4. Holocaust, Jewish (1939–1945)—Hungary.
5. Hungary—History—1918–1945.   6. Diplomats—Sweden—
Biography.   I. Title.
D809.S8W325   940.54'779439'0924   81-21161
ISBN 0-13-944322-3   AACR2
ISBN 0-13-944240-5 (A Reward book : pbk)

CONTENTS

To the memory of Maj and Fredrik von Dardel
who never gave up hope for Raoul

PREFACE

I didn't believe the story at first. I was in Stockholm on a news assignment to cover the presentation of the Nobel Prize in literature to Isaac Bashevis Singer in December 1978. In the midst of the rejoicing at a party for the author, a woman whose life had been saved as a result of Raoul Wallenberg's intervention on behalf of the Jews of Budapest in 1944 told me about the hero whose name I did not know.

The story seemed all the more improbable when she went on to explain that she was one of tens of thousands who had been saved and that the man who was responsible could still be alive in the Gulag, a prisoner of the Russians. If such a story were true, I reasoned, why didn't the whole world know it?

Since that night I have traveled to four countries in an effort to penetrate what I believe to be one of the most baffling mysteries to have arisen out of World War II. I have talked to Swedish diplomats, Hungarians who worked with Wallenberg, those who were saved by him and those who played other roles in Budapest in 1944. I have pored over official Swedish, American and Hungarian documents and personal testimonies and talked to Kremlinologists and released prisoners of the Soviet Union. This book illuminates many areas of the story, but the ultimate answers remain buried in prison files in the Soviet Union.

This book would not have been possible without the gracious cooperation of Raoul Wallenberg's half sister, Mrs. Nina Lagergren, who made Raoul's letters and school papers available to me, gave me the family photographs that appear in this book and spent many hours with me in Stockholm and New York discussing details of Raoul's life. This was supplemented by talks with Raoul's half brother, Guy von Dardel.

I am also indebted to Per Anger and Lars Berg, Wallenberg's colleagues in Budapest, for answering many questions that went outside the range of the material published in their books. Elizabeth Kasser, who worked closely with Wallenberg in Budapest, gave generously of her time and her special insight into his character. Susan Tabor, who contributed an unforgettable memoir to this book, also helped me in her role as librarian at Hebrew Union College and assisted with translation from Hungarian material.

I would like to thank the following for their assistance in translation and research: Barry Youngerman of Jerusalem, Professor Svante Hanson of Stockholm, and Katrin Tralongo of New York.

I am grateful to Professor Randolph L. Braham, director of the Jack P. Eisner Institute for Holocaust Studies of the Graduate School and University Center of the City University of New York, for reading the manuscript and offering corrections, and to the following for technical help, editorial advice and encouragement: Rosalyn Regelson, Jean Isenberg, David Gross and Philip Hochstein.

The extensive research involved in the preparation of the book was aided by a partial subsidy from the Memorial Foundation for Jewish Culture.

I am also grateful to more than fifty individuals from four continents who responded to my requests for information about their experiences in Budapest during the German occupation. Although not all of their stories appear in this text, the accumulation of varied experiences and insights helped me recreate the situation in which Wallenberg carried out his mission in Budapest. Many of these people told me their stories at great emotional cost, opening wounds that had not healed in over thirty-six years. One woman came to my office to tell me her story, but was so overcome by emotion that each time she opened her mouth to talk she had to stop. Finally she shook her head helplessly, picked up her two shopping bags and left without having said a word.

Her silence and the knowledge of Wallenberg's last "eager knockings" on the walls of his prison cell in Moscow made me aware that despite the immense accumulation of scholarship on the Holocaust and on World War II, our understanding of these cataclysmic events remains limited. We are still groping like lost ghosts in their aftermath.

Elenore Lester

FOREWORD

by Simon Wiesenthal

I first became interested in the Raoul Wallenberg story in 1967 at the request of Wallenberg's mother, the late Maj von Dardel. Since then I have been haunted by this case, and brought it up whenever I spoke to journalists over the years, asking them to talk about it and keep up a flow of information about Wallenberg's situation.

Although I have devoted many years of my life to tracking down Nazi war criminals, I consider it even more important to try to find out what has happened to Raoul Wallenberg, who is the heroic antithesis of the mass killers. Wallenberg walked into the slaughterhouse that was Budapest in 1944 and saved thousands of doomed people of all ages, ordinary citizens and children who had been pulled out of their homes to be degraded, tortured and murdered.

When the Russians marched into Budapest in January 1945, Wallenberg was happy that the atrocities would now come to an end. He went without protest with Russian soldiers to see their commander in Debrecen, but he never got there and never returned to Budapest. The Russians first said that they had him under "protection." Then they reported he was "unknown in the Soviet Union." Then, twelve years later, they reported he had died in Lubianka prison in 1947. But over the years many reports have come in from released prisoners that indicate he was alive in the Soviet Union on into the eighties.

The Russians have given contradictory and unsatisfactory accounts of this case. The family and the world have a right—in fact, a duty—to call for further investigation and clarification. Unless the Russians can give a better accounting than they have in the past, we must assume that Wallenberg remains alive in the Soviet Union.

Elenore Lester's article on Raoul Wallenberg in the Sunday *New York Times Magazine* of March 30, 1980, triggered a wave of international media interest which has been steadily building.

In Stockholm in January 1981, the thirty-sixth anniversary of Wallenberg's disappearance, we held an international seminar on the case. I was joined at the head of the panel by Gideon Hausner, the chief prosecutor of Adolf Eichmann in Jerusalem; Elie Wiesel, the chairman of the Holocaust Memorial Commission in Washington, D.C., whose entire family was deported and killed in Auschwitz before Wallenberg came to Hungary; and Ingrid Gärde-Widemar, the former Swedish Supreme Court justice. The meeting, which was held in cooperation with the International Sakharov Committee of Copenhagen, was also attended by Greville Janner, member of the British Parliament and chairman of the Raoul Wallenberg Committee of Great Britain; Andre Lwoff, the Nobel Prize-winning physicist, chairman of the Raoul Wallenberg Committee of France; Elizabeth Moynihan, secretary of the Senators' Free Wallenberg Committee of the United States; and Annette Lantos, chairman of the Raoul Wallenberg Committee of California, who along with her husband, Congressman Tom Lantos, survived the Holocaust because of Wallenberg's work in Budapest.

At the Stockholm hearing we listened to reports from former colleagues of Wallenberg's in Budapest—Per Anger and Lars Berg. We heard direct testimony from individuals who saw Wallenberg or heard of his being alive after the time he was reported dead. Nearly one-hundred representatives of the media from all parts of the world attended and reported on this testimony. We pledged ourselves to keep up the fight for information about Raoul Wallenberg.

Elenore Lester's book is an important weapon in this battle. This carefully researched work gives a vivid picture of Wallenberg's actions in Budapest and provides insight into his character. It does more. It also sets his story against the background of the events of 1944, a year when the Nazis were on the defensive, losing the war but still devoting manpower and equipment to killing Jews. However, the most terrible aspect of those events was the isolation of the Jews. Most people didn't care. Wallenberg was a rare exception—a man who could have gone on living a peaceful, comfortable life in Stockholm, but chose instead to care about his fellow humans.

That is one reason why we owe it to him not just to sit back and say it is hopeless. As long as there is a possibility that Wallenberg is alive, suffering somewhere, we must continue to work for his release. We must not leave him isolated.

The other reason we must continue the fight is simply the matter of justice. We must keep up our belief that justice will ultimately triumph, because without it we are all doomed.

ONE

A HERO VANISHES

The sky above Budapest was aflame on the frosty afternoon of January 6, 1945. The glow intensified the brightness of blood streaks in the icy Danube and tinted the snow on the rooftops and church spires a lurid orange. The air crackled with mortar and artillery fire, and huge billowing masses of flame and black smoke spotted the outskirts of the city wherever a tank had been hit. High on Castle Hill on the Buda side of the Danube, five men watched the armored divisions and artillery of the Russian Army tighten an iron vise around the city. Three of the men were husky Hungarian gendarmes bearing machine guns, trying to look as menacing as possible despite their helplessness against the chaos around them. The other two were civilians who looked about with grim detachment, as if they were immune to danger.

"How long do you think it'll be now?" the older of the two civilians asked the younger in English in a bantering, wanna-make-a-bet tone. He was in his early thirties, of medium height. His broad-brimmed hat shadowed intense dark eyes glittering in a pale, haggard face. The half smile with which he had first glanced at his companion quickly gave way to a strained tightening of the mouth.

The younger man, only nineteen, rosy with the cold, was fidgeting with the shawl around his neck; his mind seemed to be elsewhere. He shrugged and mumbled. He was secretly pressing the

1

shutter of a miniature Leica camera hidden in the folds of his heavy wool shawl. The lens was pressed against a slit in the shawl—if only he could get a shot of some Russians...

The Russians were in fact already in the northern section of Buda, but were encountering stiff resistance from the German defenders. The older man knew that if the Russians didn't soon come into Pest they wouldn't find many civilians alive. Those who weren't killed by bombs or artillery fire or crazed Hungarian Nazi thugs would surely die of disease or starvation.

Stalin had personally ordered Marshall Rodion Malinovski to take Budapest weeks earlier for "political reasons," but the Russian assault had been thrown back by the occupying Germans. The Nazi forces had been ordered by Hitler to defend Budapest as if it were Berlin. They were supported by those remnants of the Hungarian Army still willing to fight for the Hungarian Nazi government, the Arrow Cross. Thousands of Hungarian Army deserters were hiding in lice-infested cellars along with the civilians and a few German Army deserters.

It was the second week of the Russian siege of the city, and the twelfth week of a Nazi terror orgy in the streets. While the city was being pulverized, Hungarian Nazi gangs—the *Nyilas* (Arrow Cross)—roamed the streets with their machine guns, pulling the "Judeo-Bolsheviks" out of houses and hospitals and shooting them into the Danube. Hideously mutilated corpses piled up with the rubble and garbage in the streets, and here or there a body hung from a tree or a lamp post. Bodies riddled with rifle and machine-gun bullets were frozen by their blood to the ice of the Danube. Epidemics of typhus and dysentery raged. In cold and filthy cellars and bunkers throughout the city, men and women, the sick and the wounded, huddled in blankets. Women gave birth and operations were performed on kitchen tables by candlelight. Terrified, hungry and feverish children, lying in filth, whimpered and cried aloud in their sleep. The city was near famine.

A nearby burst of artillery fire sent the five men scampering back to their car in the road. They quickly piled in, the two civilians crushed between the two Arrow Cross gendarmes, who kept their machine guns poked out of the window. The third gendarme drove the car.

The older man, Raoul Wallenberg, glanced at the anxious face of the younger, then elbowed him and called attention to the way they were sandwiched between the big gendarmes.

"This reminds me of the time I was kidnapped by bandits in the States," he smiled. "I had been hitchhiking from Chicago back to school in Ann Arbor and these four guys picked me up, drove me into the forest and pulled guns. They robbed me of about fifteen dollars, I think it was."

Wallenberg smiled at the absurdity of his own comparison. He had intended to distract his companion from the dire realities of the moment, and he had succeeded in distracting himself. A quizzical smile played about his mouth as he recalled the hitchhiking escapade. That college youth would have been amazed to know that twelve years later he would be in Budapest with Swedish diplomatic papers in his pocket, rescuing Hungarian Jews from Nazis and being protected from his numerous enemies by a special guard supplied to him by a secret Hungarian Nazi contact.

The younger man nodded silently at Wallenberg's anecdote. He understood the English words, but not the context of the older man's memories. Tom Veres was nineteen, and a dedicated photographer. His hazel eyes were still glinting with amazement at the terror and beauty of the scene he had just observed. In the last year he had witnessed the German occupation of his country, bringing in horrors he could never have dreamed in his worst nightmares. The miniature Leica had caught some of those horrors. In this way he had worked with Wallenberg, trying to show the world what the Nazis were doing in Budapest. Wallenberg had sent the negatives, accompanied by his written reports, by diplomatic courier to Stockholm.

Tom had volunteered to join with Wallenberg in his efforts to save Budapest Jews, and was proud to have the skill and daring for the job. He had been trained from boyhood by his father, Paul, who had been court photographer for the Hapsburgs, monarchs of the Austro-Hungarian Empire until the end of World War I. Later Paul Veres became photographer for the new ruler of Hungary, Regent Miklós Horthy. Now a new phase of history was opening for Hungary. Tom wondered what kind of scenes he would photograph when the Russians entered Budapest. Like most Hungarians, he was not optimistic, but nothing could be worse than what the city was now undergoing.

Wallenberg lapsed back into his own thoughts. He wondered at himself for having initiated this crazy, risky excursion. In a moment of calm, after harrowing days and nights trying to wrest lives from Nazi street thugs armed with machine guns and appealing personally to whatever authorities remained in the bloody, disease-ridden city, he had impulsively turned to Tom and said, "Enough for today Let's go see where the Russians are now."

Wallenberg was afraid that if the Russians didn't move in quickly, the Nazis would blow up the ghetto with seventy thousand men, women and children in it. Adolf Eichmann, Hitler's master expediter of mass-killing, had fled Budapest before Christmas, but the SS units he had left behind were under orders to finish the job he had begun, and they were enthusiastically assisted by Hungarian Nazis. The Budapest Jews, last of the Hungarian Jews, were slated to be wiped out before the Russian entered the city.

By January 6 the Russian entrance into the city seemed imminent. At this point some Hungarian Nazis, fearing the day of reckoning when they would be tried as war criminals, tried to win favor with the Jews and the neutral legations. This was why Wallenberg was able to get guards for his excursion to Buda.

The trip from Pest to Buda across the Danube via the Chain Bridge was an escape from one bedlam into another. The bridge was supposed to be closed to all but military traffic and the most essential civilian services, but the confusion was so great that the exhausted German soldiers had stared at their car, dazed, not realizing that it had mixed-up license plates and wrong stickers. They poked grimy, bloody faces into the window, not quite knowing what they were looking for but, seeing Hungarian gendarmes with machine guns, they waved them on. Tom and Wallenberg rode up to the hill laughing at the chaos like boys on a lark.

It was a moment of release, seized from the inferno. Raoul Wallenberg was experiencing the euphoria that comes to those who narrowly escape death. He had escaped death more times than he could remember in the last months. He had stood unarmed in front of trigger-happy teenaged Hungarian Nazi thugs with machine guns and ordered them to take off—the Jews they wanted were under the protection of the Royal Swedish government, of which he was the representative. He had clambered up to the roof of a train, handing out Swedish "protection" passes to the Jews crammed into cattle cars for deportation to death camps, while Nazis fired warning shots at him. He had seized a young man from the very grip of armed Nazis, saying, "No, he is working for me." And he had sat across a dinner table from a lethally determined Eichmann, sipping brandy and urging him to give up Jew killing, since Germany had surely lost the war already.

Wallenberg received his answer from Eichmann several days later. His car, which was well known in Budapest, was rammed by a German truck and completely demolished. Neither Wallenberg nor his driver was in it.

Eichmann had called him "Jewdog Wallenberg," and the Arrow Crossmen had worse words for him. They were all fed up with his interference and wanted him out of the way. He knew because he had informers in all the camps. As a result, he had been house hopping in the last weeks. He slept in a different apartment every night to keep his enemies confused.

From the hill in Buda on January 6 it seemed that the Russian troops would be marching into the city in a matter of hours. But the stiff German resistance had been effective, and three days later the Russians had not moved forward in Buda.

On January 10, late at night, Wallenberg appeared at the Swedish legation headquarters on Gellért Hill in Buda and talked to Per Anger about the considerably worsened situation in the city. The food supply had run so low that people were exchanging pieces of valuable jewelry for a bit of bread, and a dead horse in the street brought a mob armed with knives and other implements, slicing away at the carcass. The Nazi frenzy increased, and the houses that Wallenberg had set up to provide a refuge for Jews with Swedish *Schutzpässe*, or protective passports, had been attacked by Arrow Cross gangs.

Anger and Wallenberg undertook to go together to see SS Commanding General August Schmidthuber—Anger to ask protection for the Swedish legation and Wallenberg to seek assurances that the ghetto would not be liquidated in the last hours. The Nazi general glared, unmoved, at first. But Wallenberg kept talking. His arguments made sense. The German military situation was virtually hopeless. When the war was over the general could be called to account for criminal actions. He gave no guarantees, but the message sank in.

When the interview ended Anger urged Wallenberg to come back with him to the legation and take cover there, but Wallenberg said he had to return to Pest, to keep an eye on what was happening in the ghetto. He told Anger that he had no choice: "I've taken on this assignment and I could never go home to Stockholm without knowing inside myself that I'd done all a man can to save as many Jews as possible."

The assignment Wallenberg had undertaken was for the American War Refugee Board, an agency created late in the war. As a representative of neutral Sweden, Wallenberg was able to function in German-occupied Budapest. But his Swedish diplomatic papers were, in a sense, a subterfuge. He was acting at the behest of the WRB.

For Wallenberg the assignment was a sacred mission. He was not a religious man in the formal sense, nor did he think of himself as a brave man. On the contrary, in his typically self-deprecatory manner he had referred to himself as a coward. He had never been a fighter and had always disliked competitive sports. But he had built a strong, agile body doing the things he loved—hiking, swimming, cycling, running. The stamina he had built stood him in good stead in Budapest, where lives often hung on how quickly he could move and what physical force he could project when he loped in, surprising a gang of Nazi thugs.

When Wallenberg parted company with Anger on January 10 he was, in effect, cutting himself off from diplomatic protection. In a week the German troops were to retreat to Buda, blowing up the bridges over the Danube behind them. But until then a German SS contingent and the Arrow Cross gangs continued to rule the streets of Pest. Wallenberg stood between them and the Jews. He could not prevent all the killings, but his last visit to Schmidthuber had its effect. The ghetto was never blown up.

At the end of the war Pál Szalai, a onetime Arrow Cross official who turned in the last weeks and became an informer for Wallenberg and the Jewish leaders, testified before a people's tribunal that during the last hours before the Russians moved in he learned that five hundred German soldiers and twenty-two Arrow Crossmen were planning a machine-gun massacre in the ghetto. Szalai appealed to Ernö Vajna, the minister for the defense of Budapest, to stop the action, but Vajna refused to prevent it. Szalai then went to Schmidthuber and reminded him that Wallenberg had warned that he would be held responsible for the crime after the war, and that he would be called to account not as a soldier but as a murderer.

Szalai said that Schmidthuber then summoned the Arrow Crossmen who would have commanded the operation, a German officer who would have led the Germans, Vajna, and the Budapest police commissioner, and ordered them to prevent the crime.

Wallenberg's intervention had earlier prevented thousands of deaths. In the beginning he based his rescue work upon the principle of the *Schutzpass*, a specially designed passport by which Swedish protection was extended to Hungarian Jews supposedly planning to emigrate to Sweden. There was no basis in international law for such a concept. It was a fiction the Germans were willing to accept for a time, as a matter of accommodating to circumstances which made it difficult for them to achieve their Final Solution instantaneously.

The *Schutzpass* system worked as long as there was a semblance of law and order in Budapest, but when the Arrow Cross government took over on October 15, 1944, anarchy erupted. The thugs and free-lance psychopaths who roamed the streets tried to flush out the Jews in hiding, including children protected by the churches. Wallenberg continued to press his dubious diplomatic authority for all it was worth, but more and more his power depended on his personal charisma and commando tactics. He barged in with a small group of followers screaming threats in German that he would report the gang to "higher authorities," and interposing his body between would-be killers and their victims.

Despite the threats against him, no Nazi dared take Wallenberg's life. He had developed an almost magical immunity. He had uncannily entered Nazi psychopathology, doing things that no professional diplomat, encased in a bureaucratic mind set, could have imagined or dared to do. The Nazis represented a "government" that assumed the right to kill innocent men, women and children because of their Jewish heritage. In response, Wallenberg played the role of a formal diplomat dealing precisely with the rules. If there were rules, there must be exceptions. Officially he issued fewer than five thousand *Schutzpässe*. The people who held them could not be deported. On top of the fiction of the *Schutzpass*, he imposed a deception. He actually issued about twenty thousand *Schutzpässe*, and the Nazis had no way of knowing which were "authentic" and which were not.

On top of his deception, Wallenberg superimposed an absurdity. As far as he was concerned, forged *Schutzpässe*—or any scrap of paper—had validity to save a life. He solemnly accepted old receipts and eyeglass prescriptions as temporary papers from people supposedly awaiting an official *Schutzpass*. He humored the homicidal madmen, trying to extricate as many would-be victims from their grasp as possible. Wallenberg had always admired Charlie Chaplin and the anarchic comedy of the Marx brothers. There was something of their spirit in the way he handled the Nazi bureaucracy. In Budapest he became a comedy artist functioning in a real-life catastrophe.

In the last few days before the Russians entered the Pest section of the city, the Nazi frenzy reached such a pitch that Wallenberg saw his system breaking down. He went to take cover from the marauding gangs at 16 Benczur Street. It was the elegantly appointed home of an aristocrat who had turned it over to the International Red Cross. The people living there had Red Cross protection in bringing bread and whatever other relief they could to the ghetto. Stephen Rádi, a businessman who later emigrated to New York, recalls that Wallenberg came to the house looking haggard and unshaven "like all of us," and explained that "they" were after him.

On January 13 advance Russian patrols pushed into Pest, going from house to house, entering through the cellars. They came to the Red Cross house on January 14 or 15. Wallenberg was able to greet them in Russian—he had studied it in preference to Latin in high school and was a top student in the language. According to Rádi's recollection:

The Russians very politely asked to see our identification papers. There were about twenty-five people staying at the house, and we all showed our papers. When the soldier looked at Wallenberg's he said he didn't understand and would have to call a higher officer. The higher officer looked and asked him to come with him to headquarters. Wallenberg left without taking any of his personal things. We thought he would be gone for a couple of hours, but he didn't come back for about two days.

Rádi assumed he was being held by the NKVD, the Russian security police, predecessors of the KGB, for interrogation during those two days. However, Wallenberg was actually going about his usual work in the city of horrors Budapest had become. Mrs. János Kondor of Budapest will never forget the morning or afternoon of January 16, 1945:

At that time we lived in a Swedish Embassy building at 20 Revai Street, where we had been staying for the past three weeks. There were about fifty or so tenants in the building—embassy employees and their families. We were all exhausted from the previous events: the shelling of the building, the collapse of a whole floor, etcetera. Although we had a guard at the door, a large number of Nazis with rifles seized the building. They collected all wedding rings, small chains, all remaining food, and forced us into one corner of the courtyard. In the front were Representatives Ernö Bródy and József Büchler (former members of the Hungarian Parliament), my husband and myself with our eleven-year-old son and seven-year-old daughter. In the other corner of the yard was a machine gun, facing us, and three Nazis assigned to handle the gun.

While aiming at us they shouted the worst adjectives, saying, "You rotten gangsters, you vermin, while we are protecting the country, you are hiding here. Now we will take care of you." We were standing there amidst the roaring sounds of falling bombs and Nazi abuse in dead silence. Then suddenly a group of people stormed the courtyard, led by Wallenberg. He seemed to me like an angel of mercy. He was shouting that this was an extraterritorial building. Little by little the shouting ceased, the Nazis picked themselves up and left. They left without taking what they gathered, the food, the rings, etcetera.... We could not believe our own eyes. He was victorious again, with his belief and his will power. And he left quietly. God bless him and protect him, whether dead or alive.

That was the second time Wallenberg rescued Mrs. Kondor and her family. The embassy employees she refers to were among more than four hundred people Wallenberg had taken on his personal staff. Nearly all of them were Jews, who were thus granted protection and did not have to wear the yellow star the Nazis imposed on Jews. They were free to run errands, and gather and distribute food and medicines; the young men, sometimes dressed in Nazi uniforms, guarded buildings and participated in actions like the one described by Mrs. Kondor.

When Wallenberg returned to the house on Benczur Street, the Russians had flooded the Pest side of the city and were firing straight across the Danube at Buda. Wallenberg was accompanied by his driver, Wilmos Langfelder, an engineer and a member of a distinguished Budapest family. They were in good spirits. Wallenberg gathered up his personal belongings and told George Wilhelm, who had organized the Benczur Street house, that he was going to Debrecen, about 130 miles northeast of Budapest. He planned to see the Russian commander, Marshal Rodion Malinovsky, and the heads of the newly established provisional Hungarian government.

Wilhelm didn't think Wallenberg ought to leave. There was still house-to-house fighting going on. Bursts of fire exploded in the streets throughout the day.

Wallenberg said he had to go. Through the window he pointed to the street. Outside, near his own car, were two Russian soldiers astride motorcycles. An officer sat in the sidecar of one of the motorcycles.

"They are ordered for me," he explained to Wilhelm. "I don't know whether it is to protect me or if I am under arrest."

In either case he didn't think it was a matter worth bothering about. There were more important things on his mind. He assumed he was being accompanied to Debrecen and was impatient to get there to talk about his plan for relief and rehabilitation of Budapest.

Throughout the weeks in which Wallenberg had been working day and night on rescues, he had also supervised the preparation of a plan for restoring normal life to the devastated city. His idea was to use his own staff as administrators.

In detail, his project worked out the search for lost members of families, the return of children to their parents (many had been kept hidden in convents and other religious institutions in and around Budapest, as well as in shelters); help with housing; collection and distribution of furniture (in addition to the destruction caused by bombing and shelling, Jews had been forced to leave their homes with virtually everything in them and had been packed into assigned quarters in the ghetto); help with repatriation and emigration; aid to Jews to revive the businesses that had been taken from them; care for orphans; saving of cultural values; medical care and fighting epidemics; the setting up of temporary hospitals and the planning and reconstruction of villages.

Before Wallenberg left the house on Benczur Street his old friend Lászió Petö, son of one of the leaders of the Jewish community, came over. Wallenberg invited him to join him on the trip to Debrecen, and Petö got into the car, which was being driven by Langfelder. They moved slowly through battered, icy streets filled with rubble, corpses and dead horses. Wallenberg wanted first to stop at Tátra Street.

At the Tátra Street office Wallenberg talked to Rezsö Müller, who was in charge, and to Ödön Gergely. He told them that he was going to Debrecen and would probably be gone about eight days. He said he planned to talk to the Russian High Command and the new Hungarian government, and handed Müller a large sum of money to take care of the needs of the people under Swedish protection. Langfelder and Petö waited in the car, and the Russian officer paced up and down on the sidewalk.

Wallenberg came back to the car in about fifteen minutes. By this time Petö had heard that Buda was about to fall to the Russians, and he was concerned about his parents, who had been in hiding there for months. He changed his mind about going to Debrecen, but before he left the car, it had a collision with a Russian truck. The Russian driver was furious and was ready for a violent altercation with Langfelder, but the Russian officer accompanying the car intervened and indicated that this was a diplomat's car. That ended the argument.

After Petö left, Wallenberg wanted to stop at the Swedish hospital. When the manager, Pali Nevi, saw Wallenberg's car, he hurried out to greet him and give him an account of conditions at the hospital. They walked up and down the street as they talked, and at one point Wallenberg slipped and fell on the icy sidewalk. It appeared to Nevi he had hurt himself, but he distracted attention from himself by pointing to three individuals coming out of the hospital wearing the yellow stars the Nazis had required all Jews to wear on the left breast.

"I am happy that my mission has not been completely in vain," he said, smiling, before he got back into the car.

That was the last time Wallenberg was seen by his friends in the West.

TWO

FROM THE HOT WAR INTO THE COLD

Raoul Wallenberg never got to Debrecen. What happened to him can only be pieced together from information brought back years later by released prisoners of the Russians who reported they had come into contact with Wallenberg or his driver, Langfelder, in Lubianka prison in Moscow at the end of January or early February 1945.

After Stalin's death in 1953, thousands of prisoners were released from Soviet jails. Among them were people of various nationalities who told of having sat in a cell with Wallenberg or Langfelder or of having communicated with one or the other of them through code knockings on prison walls (see Appendix). The information from three or four witnesses differs in small details, but the basic story holds. Wallenberg and Langfelder drove only a short distance to the outskirts of the city, were turned back and taken to NKVD headquarters in Budapest for further interrogation. They were then taken by train to Moscow via Rumania. They were not treated badly, and according to one report, were taken on a tour of the city and shown the Moscow subway before being brought to Lubianka and clapped into separate cells.

The day before Wallenberg left Pest the Soviet Foreign Ministry informed the Swedish legation in Moscow that Soviet patrols had found Wallenberg and were taking steps to protect him and his property. The Swedish Foreign Office (UD), therefore, had no worry about Wallenberg, but was greatly concerned about the other members of the Swedish legation. Contact with them had been cut off at Christmas time, and the UD did not learn until three months later that they had been under detention by the Russians in the countryside and were being sent home via Bucharest.

Several weeks passed without news after the first official message about Wallenberg's being held "under protection." In Stockholm, his mother, Maj von Dardel, became uneasy at not hearing from him and paid a call on Mme. Alexandra Kollontay, the Russian ambassador. She said Raoul was safe in Moscow and would be back. Shortly afterward, Mme. Kollontay invited Ingrid Günther, the wife of Foreign Minister Christian Günther, to tea and gave her the same information, with two additional details. She said it would be best if no "fuss" were made about the matter. Wallenberg was being held because he had done some "dumb" things in Budapest.

On April 17 the Swedish legation finally arrived home after having traveled by train from Bucharest via Odessa, Moscow, Leningrad and Helsinki to Åbo, Finland, and from there by ferry to Stockholm. Raoul Wallenberg's mother, hoping Raoul would be with them, was standing on the Stadsgärd quay in Stockholm with all the welcoming families. She turned away in tears when she saw that her son was not with the group.

On April 28 Raoul's distinguished banker cousin, Marcus Wallenberg, presented a written communication to Mme. Kollontay, with whom he had had friendly relations in the past, requesting her help in inquiring about Raoul.

Shortly afterward Mme. Kollontay was recalled to Moscow, and when the Swedish minister in Moscow, Staffan Söderblom, discussed the matter with her, she replied that she couldn't be of help since she was no longer connected with Swedish affairs.

The weeks grew into months and the months, years. There were rumors that Wallenberg had been killed by Nazis outside of Budapest and rumors that he was living in disguise in Buda, in Switzerland, in Istanbul. The Swedes kept inquiring and got no response. Finally, two years and eight months after Wallenberg's disappearance, Deputy Foreign Minister Andrei Vishinsky told the Swedish Foreign Office that Wallenberg "is not known in the Soviet Union." It must be assumed he either "perished during the fighting in Budapest, or was taken prisoner by the supporters of Szalasi" (chief of the Hungarian Nazi Arrow Cross government).

Nearly ten years after that (February 1957) the Soviet Deputy Foreign Minister Andrei Gromyko, responding to new Swedish inquiries, reported that "a Walenberg [name misspelled] had died of a heart attack in Lubianka Prison on July 17, 1947." The doctor who signed the report was dead, the minister for security service, Abakumov, to whom the report was addressed was dead (executed for "criminal activities") and Abakumov's chief, Beria, Stalin's head of security and top hatchet man, had also been shot for "criminal activities." The import of Gromyko's message was that Wallenberg had been a victim of Stalinist excesses. Case closed. But up to this writing dozens of reports from released Soviet prisoners and others of sightings or contacts after 1947 with a man who could have been Wallenberg have reached the Swedish Foreign Office. These have been carefully screened and some have proved to be of sufficient substance to cause the Swedish government to present the Soviet with new requests for further investigation. The Soviet government has remained adamant: Wallenberg died in 1947.

The Russians never explained why they took Wallenberg, but their motivation may be deduced from their behavior in East Central Europe during that period.

The time was three weeks before the Yalta Conference. In the minds of the general public the Big Three—Roosevelt, Churchill and Stalin—were on reasonably amicable terms as they sat down at the conference table in the Crimean resort on February 4 to make decisions about how the territories retaken from the Germans were to be apportioned and administered. V-E Day seemed close at hand, and there was good reason to feel that the alliance between the Soviet and the West had proven its success.

According to legend, the cold war did not begin until months after World War II ended. But some date it from May 12, a week after V-E Day, when Churchill warned the new American president, Harry Truman, that an "iron curtain" was descending in central Europe and said, "Surely it is vital now to come to an understanding with Russia, or see where we are with her, before we weaken our armies mortally or retire to the zones of occupation."

In actuality, the freeze was setting in as the Soviet forces swept across East Central Europe, establishing the geopolitical facts of the postwar world. Although Stalin had subscribed to the principles of the Atlantic Charter, which maintained that the Allies sought no territorial aggrandizement and would offer self-determination to the countries they liberated from the Nazi yoke, he was acting on an entirely different assumption, which he enunciated in the last weeks of the war— "Whoever occupies a country imposes his social order on it." Stalin planned to sit down at the Yalta conference table with his control already established over as much as his future sphere of influence as possible.

Churchill was at once furious and in despair about the situation. He could do nothing without Roosevelt, and Roosevelt wanted no confrontation with Stalin. Throughout the previous summer Churchill had strenuously urged Roosevelt and General Eisenhower to bring American troops into the Danube basin, but Roosevelt was opposed for political reasons and Eisenhower saw no military advantages. Roosevelt, who had from the beginning of the alliance courted Stalin and been cool toward Churchill, didn't like Stalin's growing aggressiveness, but wanted no breach in the supposed united front on the Balkan issue. He was much more concerned with the war in the Far East, for which he wanted Russian help. The atom bomb was not yet a certainty.

Although the advisers closest to Roosevelt, chiefly Harry Hopkins, had counseled a policy of catering to Stalin to win his friendship, some diplomats saw dangers in this stance. One of them was George F. Kennan, then deputy U.S. ambassador in Moscow. He wrote an anxious pre-Yalta note to Charles Bohlen, chief of the Soviet section of the U.S. State Department:

We have refused to name any limit for Russian expansion and responsibilities, thereby confusing the Russians and causing them

*constantly to wonder whether they are asking too little or whether it was
some kind of trap.*

Although Stalin used suspicion of his Allies as a weapon to
browbeat them into giving more than they wanted to, he was probably
genuinely fearful that at some moment the West would call a halt to his
territorial advances and join with the Germans in driving him back. In
retrospect this appears to be a fantastic notion, but at the time there
were forces in the American military which favored a go at the Russians.
Roosevelt's "unconditional surrender" statement after the Casablanca
Conference in January 1943 was partially intended to reassure the
Russians that there was no chance of his making a separate peace with
Germans.

Stalin's fears, or pretended fears, on this score were never
allayed. One reason for his suspicion was that he himself considered
making his own deal with the Germans. He had done it once in the
Hitler-Stalin pact of 1939, and he hinted in 1943 that he might try it again
if his partners didn't hurry up and open the Second Front.

Another reason for Stalin's suspicions was that he was aware that
some elements in Germany had been extending peace feelers to the
West for a long time. The fact is that the Germans could not believe that
the Western Allies were going to permit the Russians to gain power over
all of East and Central Europe. Some believed that by getting rid of
Hitler, they could make the deal. Hitler perceived all efforts to seek an
armistice with the West as treason, but toward the end, driven to
desperation by the fact that the Russians had reached German soil in late
January, he found hope in Reich Marshall Hermann Göring's belief that
the British would seek an armistice.

"They [the British] certainly didn't plan that we hold them off
while the Russians conquer all of Germany. ... If this goes on we will get
a telegram in a few days," Göring told Hitler on January 28.

The German generals clearly went along with that analysis.
Resistance began to collapse in the West, but stiffened on the Eastern
front. The battle of Budapest was one of the major struggles. However,
early in the spring the Germans were astounded to see American forces,
which had crossed the Elbe at considerable loss of life, turn back and
recross it in order to allow the Russians to take Berlin. A week before
the war ended when Berlin was surrounded by Russian troops, some
Germans still believed they could somehow make a deal with the West.

Heinrich Himmler made an offer to Count Folke Bernadotte chairman of the Swedish Red Cross, to surrender the Germ... the Western Allies alone. When Bernadotte tried to get back to Himmler with the negative answer, Himmler was in hiding from Hitler, who accused him of betrayal.

Despite all of Roosevelt's efforts to show good will toward the Soviet, relations between Stalin and the Western Allies became more and more abrasive during the last months of the war. Beneath the seemingly genial atmosphere of Yalta were highly disturbing problems, particularly in relation to Poland. World War II had broken out over the Nazi blitzkrieg into Poland. Now it was becoming clear that a bitter fight with Stalin was brewing over Poland. The Soviet already had firm political control over eastern Poland. The question was whether the Moscow puppet government in the East would be able to establish control of all of Poland. The non-Communist Polish leaders felt they had already been betrayed by the Western Allies, they were pressing for commitments to Polish independence. Roosevelt's failing health did not permit discussion of this crucial matter at Yalta. Some provisional agreements arranged that ultimate decisions would not be made on the matter until the war was over.

Serious trouble began to surface within weeks after the Big Three parted with a great show of cordiality at Yalta. Roosevelt came to agree with Churchill that the Soviet was reneging on the provisional agreements concerning Poland. In addition, a dispute arose between American military chiefs and the Russians over the possibility of the surrender of German troops in Italy. American diplomats wanted to start the talks without the Russians being present. Stalin accused Roosevelt of plotting a betrayal or of not knowing what was going on. In the last week of his life Roosevelt sent an indignant message to Stalin: "Frankly I cannot avoid a feeling of bitter resentment toward your informers, whoever they are, for such vile misrepresentations of my actions or those of my trusted subordinates."

Neither Roosevelt nor Churchill focussed on the fact that while one hundred eighty Russian divisions were sweeping through Europe like an avalanche, they brought with them thousands of NKVD men and political organizers. The NKVD functioned independently of the military and had the task of rooting out all political elements hostile to the Soviet or with the potential for challenging Russian autonomy. Thus, partisan groups not controlled by Moscow were eliminated as being "fascistic" or "enemies of the people." Hundreds of thousands of prisoners were taken by the troops and the NKVD. Most were sent to labor camps in Siberia to make up for the shortage caused by astronomical war casualties. Thousands of these prisoners eventually came back, and more thousands were worked and starved to death in Siberia.

Hungary got short shrift at Yalta. Despite the fact that it was one of the most anglophile of East European countries, Churchill was not much interested in it. At a special conference with Stalin in Moscow in the fall of 1944, Churchill passed Stalin a scrap of paper with some horse-trading suggestions. The Soviet could have 90 percent dominance in Rumania, but the British wanted 90 percent dominance in Greece. They could go fifty-fifty on Yugoslavia and Hungary. Stalin indicated vague agreement with the figures, but the one on Hungary was subsequently changed to a seventy-five–twenty-five power relationship. However, the exact meaning of the percentages was never spelled out. Each country seized from the Germans was to have an Allied Control Commission with representatives of the three Allies on it, but the functions of the commissions had not been clearly defined. Roosevelt was not interested in retaining an American military presence in Europe for longer than was absolutely necessary.

When the Big Three sat down at Yalta, Russian forces were in complete control of Pest and were taking Buda house-to-house. It was then clear what Stalin meant by demanding that Marshal Malinovski begin the premature assault on Budapest for "political reasons." Stalin was able to announce at Yalta that, while there was still fierce fighting in Hungary, Russian forces were in control of the situation and there was nothing to discuss. When the Allied Control Commission was set up in Hungary after the Germans were routed, the American and British representatives were treated as token figures and given little or no information or authority.

The Russians entered each country with considerable information from their agents about the various factions and individuals who might be friends or foes. It is entirely likely that zealous Russian agents in Budapest had fingered Wallenberg as an American agent with a large-scale rescue operation that might be a cover or a wedge for more extensive activities. The NKVD may have come in with orders for

Wallenberg's arrest. But even if they did not have information, they quickly found reason to interrogate him. Throughout the city they found buildings bedecked with Swedish flags, and they discovered that thousands of Hungarians carried Swedish "protection" papers. Some of these papers were forged and many of them had fallen into the hands of Nazis, who had either bought them on the black market or seized them from murdered Jews. The NKVD quickly ascertained that the man behind this confusing, and therefore suspicious, business was Wallenberg.

When they got to him for questioning he undoubtedly proved to be an extremely interesting find for agents in search of signs of possible threats to Soviet control.

First, there was the matter of Wallenberg's plan for the relief and rehabilitation of Budapest. In addition to crisis action relieving disease and starvation, he wanted to restore the economic life of the city, which included returning to the Jews their lost property and businesses. He extolled the virtues of self-help and pointed out, "We want to use the rapid routes which are offered by private action and private supervision. We will accept government and national assistance and incorporate it in our activity providing it will not cause delay in providing the assistance." He noted that he had his own staff, which he had chosen for three qualities— "compassion, honesty and initiative."

(The innocence of Wallenberg's presenting a plan for an autonomous agency in a Russian-controlled area is grimly comic viewed from the perspective of today. The plan is probably one of the items the Russian ambassador, Mme. Kollontay, had in mind when she told the Swedish Prime Minister's wife that Wallenberg had done some "dumb" things in Budapest. However, if Wallenberg was "dumb" about understanding Russian goals and methods in East Central Europe, what can be said for some of the leading statesmen of the day? In view of the fact that Wallenberg had been struggling for six months to save lives in the foulest of hells, it is understandable that he believed that when the "liberators" conquered their enemies, the first thing on the agenda would be rescue and rehabilitation of the population.)

Second, the Russians undoubtedly discovered either from Wallenberg's papers or his colleagues or from their own agents that his rescue mission in Budapest had been instigated by the American War Refugee Board. It is even possible that the Russians knew from their own agents in Stockholm that Wallenberg had been chosen for his mission by Iver C. Olsen, who represented the War Refugee Board in Stockholm, but also had connections with the Office of Strategic Services (predecessor of the CIA). Wallenberg may have been totally unaware of Olsen's OSS connections, but from a Russian point of view Wallenberg could be viewed as an American agent using Swedish diplomatic papers and a humanitarian mission as a cover for establishing an American presence in Hungary. It was not yet clear that the Americans had little interest in Hungary.

Third, the Russians were interested in the large amounts of money Wallenberg had at his disposal. (His colleagues were interrogated intensively on this point.) Wallenberg probably tried to avoid answering, pleading diplomatic immunity, but eventually the Russians undoubtedly learned that the money came from the WRB, the American Jewish Joint Distribution Committee (an agency designed to aid needy Jewish communities throughout the world) and the Hungarian Jews who were not allowed, under the Nazis, to hold money or valuables beyond the barest stipend. Wallenberg could have no idea of how sinister the combination of American and Jewish money looked in Russian eyes. Stalin had yet to reveal the full extent of his paranoia about Jews and their connection with "Wall Street" and "imperialism." In his purge of "Jewish cosmopolitans" in the intelligentsia and political circles before his death in 1953, Stalin was to name the "Joint" as an organization set up by American intelligence to "conduct extensive espionage, terrorist and other subversive work in many countries including the Soviet Union." As early as 1948 Stalin launched an anti-Jewish campaign in Soviet bloc countries by associating the words Zionism, cosmopolitanism and Nazism.

Fourth, Wallenberg consorted regularly with top German and Hungarian Nazis. That was how he got information about what they were up to so he could short-circuit their plans, and how he made deals to save people. But the standard accusation the Soviet police made against individuals or groups they were out to get was that they had consorted with Nazis. They arrested thousands who had tried to contact relatives in Nazi-held territories. The fact that Stalin himself had made one world-shaking deal with Hitler, and threatened a second, evidently had no bearing on the matter.

Fifth, his name was Wallenberg. The Russians undoubtedly quickly ascertained that their man was a member of one of Sweden's wealthiest and most illustrious families. The Wallenbergs were not only the leading bankers of Sweden, with holdings in all of the major industries and most of the largest corporations, but they had negotiated all of Sweden's trade dealings to both Allies and Nazis during the war. Marcus Wallenberg had headed the Swedish trade mission to Great Britain, and his brother Jacob handled the same job in Germany. Thus Raoul Wallenberg was related to the man who had been chiefly responsible for selling the Germans the ball bearings that were the life blood of the German war machine. The fact that Marcus and Jacob were second cousins of Raoul's and that his contacts with them had been limited would not be important to Russian interrogators trying to penetrate to the powers behind the individuals they suspected.

To make matters even more complex and suspicious from a Russian point of view, Jacob Wallenberg was a good friend of Karl Goerdeler, the Lord Mayor of Leipzig, who had been hanged by the Nazis after the failure of an assassination attempt on Hitler on July 20, 1944. From 1941 on, Goerdeler had been a leader in anti-Hitler conspiracies and tried to keep the lines open to Britain to negotiate peace if Hitler were overthrown. Evidently, Goerdeler had long had the idea that a separate peace could be made—and if it were to be made, what more likely links could there be than Jacob and Marcus Wallenberg?

Finally, what was the cousin of Jacob and Marcus Wallenberg *really* doing in Budapest? To The Russians, who had seen more than a million Jews massacred in their own territory and who by the end of the war were to have a total of some twenty million dead, the idea that a leading Swedish capitalist was sitting in bloody Budapest in the midst of a fierce war, risking his life to save a handful of Hungarian Jews, must have seemed absurd. Worse, it was sinister.

Wallenberg's mission to save Jews may also have seemed to the Russians to be related to another rescue effort the Soviets had helped to scotch. In the late stages of the war, while the gas chambers at Auschwitz were working at peak levels, offers to release some Jews for ransom came through a number of sources. In June 1944, shortly before Wallenberg was chosen for his mission, two such offers reached the West and were interpreted as coming directly from Heinrich Himmler, who had built his own empire within the Nazi hierarchy. One of the offers was funneled from Eichmann in Budapest through Jewish underground sources to London and Washington. It involved a deal to exchange a million Jews for "winterized" trucks to be used only on the Eastern front. Diplomatic analysts perceived this as a preliminary to opening "separate peace" talks.

Jewish leaders hoped that discussions would be opened simply in order to stall the exterminations. Since the war had taken a decisive turn against the Germans, there was a possibility that it would end abruptly and lives would be spared. However, Roosevelt, British Prime Minister Winston Churchill and Foreign Minister Anthony Eden agreed that the Russians must be consulted on the matter. The Russians were, as expected, unequivocally opposed to any such discussions, and there the matter ended.

Roosevelt and the British may have intended to demonstrate to Stalin their honest commitment to him by exposing this proposal. However, it is possible that their frankness served to alert him to the possibility that such tactics were being tried by the Germans. Wallenberg had come to Budapest immediately after the Jews-for-trucks deal had been exposed to the Russians and rejected. He had remained there throughout the Nazi occupation. The Russians would certainly have wanted to investigate the possibility that he could have been involved in some clandestine discussions with the Nazis. Could his rescue operation have been a cover for "separate peace" negotiations?

The cruel deception involved in the manner in which Raoul Wallenberg was spirited away by the NKVD was typical of Soviet methods of handling prominent individuals they wanted out of the way as they took over the East European countries. The same type of deception was practiced three months later in the removal of sixteen political and military leaders of the underground Polish government, many of whom had fought the Nazis throughout the war and had participated in the Warsaw uprising of the previous fall. The Poles emerging from their forest hideouts were invited to lunch to "talk things over" with General Ivanov. Although they had some misgivings, they got on a plane to Moscow. There they were met with limousines, given a tour of the city, including the Moscow subway, then driven to Lubianka prison and shut behind bars. They were brutally interrogated day and night for months before all but one confessed to being traitors and "enemies of the people." The famous Soviet-style "confessions" served to justify the quashing of all dissent. They were sentenced to long terms.

It is interesting to note that the day Wallenberg stepped into his car to go to Debrecen with his Russian escorts, the Soviet forces were marching into the rubble of Warsaw and the leaders of the anti-Russian Polish nationalists were hiding from both Germans and Russians in the forests of Poland. That week the Red Army began the winter offensive which was to leave the Soviet in control of East Central Europe to the present day.

In retrospect it seems incredible that a Swedish diplomat on a mission for the American government could be spirited off to a Soviet jail without its causing the slightest stir in the West. But the war was drawing to a close, the fighting was still fierce, the death camps were opened up and the entire continent was a chaos of epidemics, destroyed cities, corpses and distraught refugees. A lost Swedish diplomat merited no more than a dozen paragraphs in *The New York Times* of April 26, 1945.

However, the officials of the War Refugee Board, who had sent Wallenberg on his mission and knew how magnificently he had performed, notified Secretary of State Cordell Hull, who in turn instructed Ambassador Harriman in Moscow to offer American support to Swedish inquiries into Wallenberg's disappearance. Swedish Minister Söderblom declined the offer. The Swedish government was in the process of adjusting to the fact that its neighbor to the East was emerging from the war as an exceedingly powerful country with which it would want to remain on the best of terms. Minister Söderblom did not want to make a big issue of the case. Reports released from the Swedish Foreign Office many years later showed that from the earliest stages of the case, Söderblom was more than willing to accept the rumor that Wallenberg had been killed outside of Budapest.

Shortly after the end of the war, Sweden elected a Social Democratic government which was even more eager to maintain good relations with the Soviet Union. Out of sympathy for the "Marxist experiment," many in the government believed that the Wallenberg case created an unnecessary sore spot and wished to bury it. It was not until 1980, when a large batch of foreign office secret papers were opened up, that an aroused Swedish public was able to learn how inadequate were the gestures made on Raoul Wallenberg's behalf. The newspaper *Aftonbladet* referred to government mishandling of the case in the early years as amounting to a "betrayal" of Raoul Wallenberg. Tage Erlander, retired Swedish prime minister, expressed chagrin at Sweden's failure to act effectively on behalf of "one of the greatest Swedes of our time," and encouraged continued efforts because "It is very likely that he is alive."

THREE

THE EDUCATION OF AN UPPER-CLASS SWEDE

In all logic, one could expect the Russians to question why an upper-class Swede was risking his life in bloody Budapest, trying to rescue a few thousand Hungarian Jews. Wouldn't anyone wonder why this man of privileged background would devote himself so passionately to saving a doomed group of people? He could have left without feeling disgraced when anarchy erupted in the city. A diplomat by definition deals with normal governments, not street gangs and cold-blooded killers. What uncanny inner resources did he possess that enabled him to face thugs with machine guns without flinching? What spiritual wellsprings led him to Budapest when he was in the fortunate position of living in one of the few countries of the world free of war or occupation?

The answers are buried deep in the mysteries of character, but some insight can be gleaned from an examination of his life and family background.

Up to 1936, no one could have predicted for Wallenberg anything but a supremely happy life, aloof from the dark turbulence of the world. But that year he came to a sudden self-recognition. The sign of it appeared in a small paragraph in a letter to his grandfather from Haifa, where he was working as a clerk in the Holland Bank:

To tell the truth I don't feel especially bankish; a bank president should have something judgelike and calm about him and moreover be cool and cynical. Freund [Raoul's boss] and Jacob W. [his cousin] are no doubt typical and I myself feel as different from them as I possibly could. I think it is more in my nature to work positively for something than to sit around telling people, no.

Raoul was then about to turn twenty-four. He was more than a year out of architecture school and was chafing against his grandfather's plans for him. Gustaf, the retired Swedish ambassador to Turkey, was living in Istanbul; he had gotten Raoul his job in Haifa as a first step in the banking career he planned for his grandson. Gustaf, once ambassador to China and Japan, had a long-cherished dream of founding an international bank designed to promote trade with Sweden. Raoul would head it. They had talked about it for years.

The projected head of the dream bank was, in 1936, living in an inexpensive, strictly kosher pension populated mainly by refugees from Hitler's Germany. It was a place, Raoul reported, in which "One eats with one's hat on, and only milk and vegetables are served on the Sabbath."

Raoul had no complaint with the pension, which in fact was a cozy, popular place at 18 Arlosorof Street, filled with middle-class German Jews who were as disoriented in British-mandated Palestine as Raoul. The pension was run by the sister-in-law of a noted artist and religious Zionist, Herman Struck. It was cheaper, warmer and livelier than the alternative—the places occupied by British colonial officials, who despised "natives" in general and had no love for either Arabs or Jews.

Raoul's complaint to his grandfather was simply that he was not getting anywhere because he was headed in the wrong direction. Up to this point he had readily accepted his grandfather's guidance. Raoul's father had died of cancer at age twenty-three, three months before Raoul was born. Young Raoul inherited the love and dreams Gustaf had for his only son. Raoul grew up to resemble his father in vitality; seriousness of purpose combined with a sense of humor; an open, happy outlook; and artistic talent.

When Raoul was six, his mother, Maj, an exquisite and vibrant woman, married Fredrik von Dardel, a lawyer involved in health services who later became head of the Karolinska Institute, Sweden's great medical research center. A year after Maj's remarriage, Raoul acquired a half brother, Guy, and two years later his sister Nina was born.

Although Raoul was very much a part of a warm, close family and had a devoted stepfather, he remained a Wallenberg. And to be a Wallenberg in Sweden was no trivial matter. It is one of the best-known names in the country. Sweden's top standard of living today owes much to the enterprise of the Wallenberg family.

The earliest known Wallenbergs were Jacob, a seaman who in the mid-eighteenth century wrote Sweden's first realist classic, *Min Son På Galjen* (*My Son the Sailor*), based on his adventures in East Asia in the 1760s, and his brother, Marcus, a lector (reader of church services) in Linköping. Marcus's son became bishop and a lawyer with financial talent. He was a stockholder in Göta Channel in northern Sweden and thought the state mishandled it. He wound up owning it.

It was Marcus's oldest son, André Oscar, who took a step that helped move Sweden decisively into the rank of the world's most advanced industrial democracies. André Oscar began his career by going to sea at age fifteen, and went on to become captain of Göta Channel's first steamer. Then he went into business in Sundsvall. He was elected to Sweden's lower house of parliament, the Riksdag, in 1853, and served until his death in 1866.

During his years as a seaman, A.O., as he came to be known, visited New York and became excited by the new world of finance he saw there. He wanted to start a modern commercial bank. In 1856, at the age of forty, he realized his dream and founded the Enskilda Bank.

Up to that time Sweden was one of Europe's poorer countries, but in the mid-nineteenth century it was ready for a huge industrial breakthrough. A big spurt in population growth in Western Europe created a demand for timber. Norway was no longer able to meet the demand, but Sweden had vast acres of virgin forest. The steam engine afforded the opportunity for speedier delivery of logs to mills.

The year the Enskilda Bank opened, the country's first railroad got started. A.O. saw the opportunity for the bank to further new developments by encouraging the use of savings for constructive purposes. He wanted to finance new enterprises, dispensing advice along with the money. He was fearless (some felt too fearless) about borrowing abroad and issuing notes and bonds. He accepted partial ownership in the wide variety of corporations, and often helped build a business, then withdrew from it and went on to the next enterprise. The only company he owned completely was Asea, the electric firm, which he wanted to be sure of keeping in Swedish hands.

One of A.O.'s great achievements was to establish good relations with foreign banks, and these relations were continued by his sons, Knut, Gustaf, Oscar, Axel and Marcus. When A.O. died, Knut (K.A.) took over the management of the bank, but he soon gave way to the youngest, Marcus, and went into diplomacy. He was Sweden's foreign affairs minister during World War I. Axel was ambassador to the United States in the twenties. Marcus proved to be the financial wizard of the family; it was he who shaped a financial empire with holdings in steel, iron ore, ball bearings, timber, blast furnaces, forest reserves, communications and hydroelectric plants. Enskilda helped finance Gustaf de Laval, the inventor of the revolutionary cream separator. It was behind the railway that opened up the rich Arctic iron-ore fields, the beginnings of Scandinavia's pulp and paper industry and the fleets that carried Swedish exports abroad.

Marcus, Sr., strictly adhered to the family motto, *Esse, non Videri*, "To be, not to be seen." It suited his reclusive nature, and he became known as "the Judge." He trained his sons, Jacob and Marcus, Jr., to carry on his empire. This they did most successfully until Jacob died at the age of eighty-seven in 1980. Marcus, seven years younger, was still playing tennis at the age of eighty. He was Sweden's tennis champion in the twenties.

Raoul's grandfather Gustaf was of a different temperament from his younger brother Marcus. An expansive man, strongly interested in people, he was keenly aware of Swedish insularity. He found a suitable outlet for his interest in other cultures by focusing on trade. He initiated the Trellebor-Sassnitz ferry route, which became important in trade with Germany, and he developed Sweden's East Asiatic Steamship line.

In 1900 Gustaf (G.O.) became a Liberal party member of the Riksdag, and during this period he promoted the importance of Sweden's exporting to the not-yet-exploited markets of the Far East. In 1906 he was appointed Sweden's first envoy to Tokyo, and the following year he was also accredited to Peking. He aggressively pursued Sweden's trade interests in China and was particularly interested in establishing Swedish leadership in China's telephone systems. However, World War I interfered with his plans.

In 1920 Gustaf accepted appointment as Swedish minister in Constantinople. It was an exciting assignment for a man of Gustaf's background and outlook. With the breakup of the old Ottoman empire at the end of World War I, Turkey needed to make drastic internal changes in order to survive. The nation found its leader in Kemal Ataturk, who revolutionized every aspect of Turkish life from 1923, when he became first president of the Turkish republic, until he died in 1938. Gustaf witnessed the transformation of Turkey from a medieval Islamic country to a modern democracy. The educational system was secularized, women were given voting rights and brought into the political arena, the metric system was introduced, the language was modernized and the first railways were constructed.

Gustaf became an enthusiast of the new Turkey and vigorously championed favorable trade relations with Sweden. He felt so comfortable in Istanbul (formerly Constantinople) and was so honored there that he preferred to remain when he retired in 1930.

Raoul's heritage on the maternal side was also rich in creative energies. His maternal great-great-grandfather, Michael Benedicks, was one of the first Jews to settle in Sweden at the end of the eighteenth century. He converted to the Lutheran Church, married a Christian woman and they had nine children. He was a jeweler and quickly rose to become the court jeweler to King Gustav III. He later became financial adviser to Karl Johann XIV, the king who had once been Count Bernadotte, Napoleon's marshal. Many of Benedick's nine children distinguished themselves in business or the arts. His granddaughter Sophie, Raoul's grandmother, married Sweden's first neurosurgeon, Dr. Per Wising.

Maj Wising, the youngest of four beautiful daughters, was the tomboy of the family. At eighteen she was full of life and fun. When Raoul Wallenberg, Sr., then a twenty-one-year-old naval officer, met her, he was immediately smitten. He wrote to his parents in Tokyo: "She is lovely, extremely serious and ambitious, but also gay"; "She is intelligent—she listens well"; "She is healthy. She can walk 30 kilometers [about eighteen miles] in one afternoon without tiring."

The romance was approved by both sets of parents and the young couple was married. The cream of Swedish society turned out for the elegant wedding dinner at the Grand Hotel in Stockholm on September 27, 1911.

Three months later Maj was pregnant, and Raoul developed the cancer which was to take his life on May 10, 1912, eleven days before Maj's twenty-first birthday. Raoul Gustaf was born on Sunday, August 4, with a caul on his head, considered by some to be an omen of a great destiny. Maj refused an anesthetic for the birth. She said she wanted to be awake to experience it.

For the next few months Maj was torn between anguish and joy. She saw her husband's face in her baby and she struggled constantly to overcome the depression that at times overwhelmed her. She was breast-feeding and feared that her pain might harm the baby. She wrote frequently to her parents-in-law in Tokyo in her precise delicate hand, on paper with wide black borders, about her feelings of "powerlessness against that cruel death that has taken everything, everything from me." She told of her fears that she would be unable to bring up her young son alone.

Just as Maj was beginning to conquer her grief, another tragedy struck. Professor Wising one day returned from his work at the hospital, exhausted and feverish. Within a couple of days he was dead of pneumonia. Again, Maj struggled against her grief, fearful of its effect on her baby. Now she had to comfort her mother as well.

The baby Raoul became the center of the world for the two bereft women. There were sad years, but they were brightened by Raoul's growth into vigorous childhood. Maj wrote to her in-laws about Raoul's first tooth, his first steps, his first words. When he was four she could write joyously, "He is as rosy as an angel. You should see how he struggles to reach the top of the hill with his sled."

A new happy life began with Maj's marriage to von Dardel. Raoul was now one of a family. He had a passion for ships and planes and knew all the World War I battleships. He loved construction and insisted on visiting all the spots in Stockholm where new building was going on. He would watch and talk to the engineers about what they were doing. He was also intensely interested in business and collected reports about various corporations, including the Wallenberg enterprises. He discussed what they were doing and tried to figure out what he would do if he had control. At ten he decided to read Sweden's classic encyclopedia, *Nordisk Familjebok*, from A to Z. According to his mother, he got through it. When his grandfather came home to Stockholm on visits they discussed world affairs together like two adults.

When Raoul was twelve, Grandfather Gustaf asked to have him sent on a visit to him in Istanbul by train. A conductor was supposed to keep an eye on him all the way, but somewhere en route from Belgrade the train stopped because of a political demonstration and Raoul got out to see what was going on. He was missing for a couple of hours until the conductor managed to find him. Raoul became accustomed to travel— he spent vacations visiting friends or relatives in Germany, France and England, and often took trips with his Wallenberg grandparents.

Raoul attended the New Elementary School, a high quality public school in Stockholm, from ages nine through seventeen. He quickly distinguished himself there. Although he was strong and vigorous, he disliked competitive sports. He loved hiking and swimming. His flaxen baby hair had turned dark and wavy and he had big, intense dark eyes, which at times turned inward, lost in thought. He enjoyed sketching and enthusiastically made posters for all school events. He was an excellent debater. He studied German, French and English. He disliked Latin and Greek and believed they were useless. In his late high school years he was one of five in a class of 40 to study Russian. He thought it would be more useful for the future than other languages.

In Sweden it is traditional for graduating high school seniors to celebrate with large dinner parties and then enjoy a month of high-jinks. They wear white caps, and everyone smiles indulgently at their capers. This free period represents a last fling at adolescence before the youngsters metamorphose into morose adult Swedes.

Raoul would have none of this. He had a small dinner party and went to work in the Enskilda Bank the week after graduation. However, he had to leave for a year of military service before college. It was family tradition to go into the navy. When Raoul received his preinduction examination, he discovered for the first time that he was blind to the color red. Yet his artwork was so good, this flaw was never noted.

Raoul therefore enlisted in the army and set out to be a first-rate soldier. He had no appetite for ordinary soldiers' diversions, but on the other hand, he didn't think much of the authorities who made a big issue about occasional drunkenness. When two culprits were caught and sentenced to jail, he arranged a feast for them, and he and his friends carried them to jail on golden chairs.

Raoul's lively humor was zany and satirical. Ingemar Hedenius, who later became a noted classics and philosophy professor at Uppsala University, spent a happy period with Raoul in a military hospital. The two young men were not so ill that they couldn't talk and laugh from early morning to late at night. Hedenius recalled:

We composed songs, which I am sorry to say were perhaps more obscene than really funny. He created the words and I the music. We were absolutely open to each other about our sentiments and views of life. We belonged, both of us, to the upper class, and he seemed to me to be more proud of his family than I was of mine. I was left-wing at that time; he was not. He spoke of himself as "a Wallenberg and an eighth-part Jew" and seemed to regard this as a guarantee of success in life. (Actually, Wallenberg was only one-sixteenth-part Jewish.)

The two boys dreamed together of starting a great daily newspaper

which would outclass all competitors in Sweden. Raoul would be the owner, the manager and the chief editor of that enormous newspaper, and he was eager to appoint me the chief political and cultural columnist. If we only continued our friendship we should have had a deciding influence on practically everything in our country.

After his army service, Raoul was shipped off to the University of Poitiers for the summer. Gustaf felt it was a good place for Raoul "to learn the basics of the excellent French spoken in central France." He served another six-week stint in the army before setting out by ship for the University of Michigan's school of architecture. But first he took a trip around the United States.

Raoul immediately loved the relaxed American style, and took to wearing sneakers, eating hot dogs and hitchhiking everywhere. No cars were allowed on campus, and many of the students worked part-time all the way through college. The school had an excellent reputation, but most of the students came from families that couldn't afford to send them to the more prestigious eastern schools.

Gustaf approved Raoul's desire to study architecture. His first goal was to mold his grandson into a well-rounded man who could relate to people from all walks of life and from all cultures. Later he would be trained for banking. Raoul was happy with the plan—at least the first part of it.

Raoul quickly distinguished himself by his talent, his dedication to his studies, his openness and charm. Most of his fellow students became aware that he belonged to an important Swedish family, but they had no concept of the magic of the Wallenberg name in Sweden. Few of them had ever traveled outside of the United States, and they were impressed with Raoul's knowledge of architecture in various parts of the world. Raoul lived, as did most students, first in a modest room in the architecture fraternity house and later, in a boarding house near the campus. One student recalls that Raoul painted a mural depicting a lush tropical landscape on brown wrapping paper and hung it in his room. Raoul's art professor, John Slusser, was not aware of his color blindness, but only of his talent. When he inquired whether Raoul had considered going into painting as a career, he recalls that the young man said he expected to follow his family's tradition and go into banking.

Raoul's broad range of interests and good command of English were revealed in a series of college compositions. In one he discussed the events that led up to World War I. In another he analyzed the problems of industrialization and recommended that workers should have more say in the running of enterprises and that they should have shares in the company. This, he said, would lead to greater productivity. He discussed architecture and the vogue then for "historic styles," stating that although he was opposed to copying the past, "The mere fact that a thing exists shows that there is or has been some good reason for it—it is a marvelous source of inspiration."

In one essay he examined Stalin's Five Year Plan and commended it. He believed that Stalin had given "a great people the possibility to live and develop itself. The Russians had caught sight of their national force." He recognized that the plan called for great sacrifices; he compared the Russians to early Christians as against the apathetic Romans around them. Without comparing Sweden to Rome, he noted that in May of 1930, Russia sold as much lumber as Sweden had in the entire preceding year. He pointed out that lumber accounted for two thirds of Sweden's export. He urged Sweden to try to recover what had been lost to the Russians, suggesting that the country reach out, as it did in 1905, to markets in China, India, South America and the Balkans.

"The whole world moves forward and those who do not move with it remain behind and disappear," he warned darkly.

The architecture program was very demanding and there was little time for social life, but Raoul was immensely popular and stood out at parties for his charm, humor and gracious manners.

Raoul's fellow students were not aware that he was spending a large portion of his free time with Bernice Ringman, a young woman of Swedish background, who was an instructor at the Michigan State Normal College (now Eastern Michigan University) in Ypsilanti, five or six miles from Ann Arbor. Bernice was a physical therapist working with a pioneer in special education, developing programs for handicapped children. Raoul admired Bernice's devotion to her work and often met her in the late afternoons to help her with the children. When she had to bring the children from the hospital to their homes, he would often carry those unable to walk.

Bernice recalls that Raoul sketched constantly and that he tried to teach her as much as possible about his work. They attended concerts frequently and they both particularly enjoyed Handel's *Messiah* each year (Raoul had a fine voice and sang *Messiah* in the church choir in Stockholm).

Despite their serious concerns the young couple went to see Laurel and Hardy comedies whenever they could. ("Raoul laughed throughout and talked about them afterward," she said.) They also traveled to Detroit to see Fred Astaire in the musical comedy, *Roberta*.

Raoul also hitchhiked to Detroit with a fellow student, Frederic James, to see ballet or hear a concert.

"I remember that he loved music," reports James. "He and I would go to the music department of the university and listen to records. Mozart opera was our favorite."

James also recalls bull sessions at which Raoul was a "star." "He always thought through to the essence." Above all, James recalls him as being "full of energy, good humor and generally a good guy."

Another fellow student, Ernst L. Schaible, remembers that Raoul enjoyed "fabricating new words to help describe an object or explain a situation. One instance I particularly remember: On a warm spring day in Ann Arbor, as we were climbing a stair, a shapely coed in a summer dress passed us on her way down. We were both struck by her grace and beauty as she bounded down those stairs, and Raoul remarked that he admired the 'kunkling' of her breasts."

Lyman E. Woodward remembers that Raoul once cycled about sixty miles from Ann Arbor to the Woodward home in Owosso, Michigan.

"My mother was extremely impressed by this bright foreign student and invited him to speak on Swedish art and architecture at her study club and Raoul was happy to comply. Although he had arrived with his clothes in a knapsack, when he appeared for his lecture at the Women's Club he wore striped pants and a cutaway jacket with a bat-winged collar, and of course the good ladies of Owosso were charmed."

One can only guess that Raoul, deciding that his clothes from the knapsack would not do, went out and rented a dress suit.

Neither Raoul's fellow students nor his teachers became aware of Raoul's color blindness, but he was concerned about it and felt that it could weaken his work as an architect. He decided to study construction engineering during his first year, but found that this called for a mathematical aptitude he lacked. He switched to the architecture program, but he wrote to his mother, "I make rather dreadful mistakes all the time."

Raoul did not return to Stockholm during his college years. He spent his vacations traveling about the United States and Canada. He often visited an aunt, his mother's sister, who lived in Greenwich, Connecticut. She had married Colonel William Calvin, American military attaché to the Scandinavian countries during World Wars I and II. Raoul enjoyed seeing his cousins, who were close to his age. One of them, later Mrs. Lucette Kelsey, recalls that

Raoul's luggage, filled with laundry, always arrived first. He came by bus or hitchhiked, which my mother didn't like. We had wonderful times doing the things young people did—going on picnics, swimming, dancing, going to movies. Raoul was so much fun, a wonderful mimic. He liked to deliver speeches of various ambassadors in their own language or in a made-up language if he didn't know their language—like the Chinese ambassador. He was particularly good at the pompous German ambassador. He had us in stitches.

During the summer of 1933, Raoul worked at the Swedish exhibition of the Chicago World's Fair. He stayed at the YMCA and sweltered through one of the city's hellish heat waves. He earned three dollars a day, keeping glassware and porcelain in merchandising order. On his way home to Ann Arbor he had the adventure he would recall ten years later on the fiery night in Budapest. He had gotten a ride in a fine car with a gentleman who sped along at seventy miles an hour and had to brake suddenly at a train crossing. The car was damaged badly, but neither the driver nor Raoul was hurt. The driver had to be towed away and Raoul was left to thumb his way along the highway, carrying two suitcases. When four men offered to pick him up, he accepted.

Raoul wrote to his mother about how the men, who "didn't look at all nice," began asking him how much it would be worth to take him all the way to Ann Arbor. He said he didn't have any money or he wouldn't be hitchhiking. Finally the car swerved off the highway and rode into a side road in a forest.

I was told to get out of the car. One of them had a revolver so I obeyed. They asked for money and I gave them what I had, even what I had in the luggage in an envelope. Maybe it was stupid to reveal that I had money in the suitcase, but I have heard so much how they search you and leave you naked on the highway that I felt it was better to cooperate. At least I hung on to $13 in my pocket.

After they got their money, Raoul asked not to be left in the forest, but to be brought back to the highway. The robbers agreed to do this and piled his suitcases on top of him in the car so that he couldn't move.

During the entire period I felt no fear. It seemed like an exciting, adventurous cops and robbers game. My unusual calm caused them concern. They became worried about a trap and this suddenly led them to put me out into a ditch from the still-moving car. They threw my luggage after me. In the morning I found some railroad tracks and stopped a local train. This took me 200 miles from Ann Arbor where I reported my adventures to the police.

I immediately decided I will not stop hitchhiking because of this incident, but I will learn to be more clever and will take less money along. It is my feeling that in this instance I was too naive handing over the money from my luggage. They were amateurs and would probably have been satisfied with the money from my pocket. This is what I learned from the whole affair.

Perhaps Raoul was even more naive in not understanding the consternation the story would cause his mother, nearly ten thousand miles away. However, it is evident that he enjoyed the adventure. He was also clearly driven by a need to analyze and share his experience, to find clues to the behavior of others, to understand his own reaction in both its weakness and strength, and to stow the information away for reference for a future he could not envision.

Devotion to his architectural studies did not prevent Raoul from keeping an eye on business and political affairs with the intensity of one who assumes a leadership role in relation to them. In a 1934 letter to his mother, he wrote that since he came to the United States, he had been thinking about whether it would be desirable to create an open border between the three Scandinavian countries, and he had studied statistics to see if there is any direct economic basis for a union. He found that, unfortunately, this was not the case. Nevertheless, he felt it would be an advantage from a political point of view because "the more turbulent Europe becomes, the more necessary it is to make the machinery of production cheaper at home."

Raoul also questioned whether skyscrapers would be desirable for Stockholm and decided they would make no economic sense—and asked to have Guy mail him the latest reports of the Wallenberg enterprises.

In a letter to his grandfather he reported on Swedish-American trade. On his initial trip around the United States in 1932, he interviewed Swedish businessmen in various parts of the country, probably at his grandfather's suggestion.

He discovered that "the Swedes of Minnesota have acquired a reputation for stupidity, but no such thing is evident in the Swedes in Washington and Oregon." He noted that those states are two of the most popular in the country:

For a Swede to come from the old country and not show proper respect is like a slap in the face. The Swedes and descendants of Swedes there show a large and whole-hearted interest in things Swedish. They are easy to flatter and the finest flattery they can get is to tell them that they have built a fine country. If that ritual is observed they are more willing to buy and sell Swedish things, other things being equal. They felt not enough economic support is given their loyalty. I often heard complaints that small Swedish-American firms selling Swedish goods on the American market fail because of the difficulty of obtaining credit from the banks to finance these deals. Efforts were made to create Swedish-American banking institutions on the West Coast, but companies have disappeared in this and previous crises.

Raoul took a keen interest in the American political scene as he did in all aspects of American life. One of his former schoolmates recalled that he had spent one of his school holidays in Washington, D.C., exploring the governmental process.

At the time of Raoul's arrival in the United States a hot political contest was going on between President Herbert Hoover and challenger Franklin Delano Roosevelt. Raoul studied the platforms of the Republican and Democratic parties and discovered that there was actually little difference between them. However, his Swedish sense of propriety was shocked at the American style of political debate: "It impresses a foreigner unfavorably to hear the different candidates being assailed as crooks and imbeciles by their respective foes."

Raoul never developed any strong sympathy for the Left, but he was always careful to examine what they had to offer. He was impressed by Norman Thomas's reputation for honesty and noted that he was expected "to draw a large vote, not only from radicals and unemployed, but from those who have become tired of the graft and inefficiency displayed by both Republicans and Democrats." He added that, "It is whispered that Thomas is supported by the Republican Party in order to take the radical votes that Roosevelt would otherwise get." He expressed disbelief that a man with Thomas's record for honesty would permit such shenanigans.

These are not letters from a young man being forced against his will to take an interest in business and political matters. Raoul was excited by business and brought creative energies to his study of it. One may assume that when he indicated to his art professor that he expected to follow the family tradition, it was not with any profound regret. Evidently he had not yet realized that there might be a conflict within him between the sensitive, morally aware artist and the hardheaded businessman. Filled with youthful energy and ambition, he thought he could harness his artistic endeavors to commercial enterprise. Certainly, the field of architecture was a likely place for the two to meet.

Raoul completed his studies at Ann Arbor in three and a half years, and walked off with the top award in his class, a medal from the American Institute of Architects. He then bought a jalopy and set out with a friend for a trip to Mexico and a visit to his Aunt Nitsa. She was his father's sister and had been named Sassnitza after Gustaf's Trellebor-Sassnitz ferry service. Her daughter Gite, although only eight at the time, remembers that visit well: "I adored him. He could imitate around twenty-five animals. He paid a lot of attention to me and tried to teach me to play chess. He was so much fun!"

Raoul paid for his expenses on the Mexico trip by doing sketches of the farmhouses and countryside and selling them to people in the areas he passed through.

Raoul traveled home to Sweden by boat; on his way home he designed a plan for a new recreational center. The center was to be built on a quay in front of Stockholm's town hall and court of appeals, and it was to include a swimming pool and museum. The design later won second prize in a contest in which dozens of well-known architects competed. Unfortunately, it was never built.

Before going to Stockholm, Raoul visited his grandparents in Nice. Gustaf was by this time ailing, but he had arranged a job for Raoul in Capetown, South Africa. Gustaf wanted Raoul to be close to a small business, where he could study the workings from the ground up. So for six months Raoul traveled the length and breadth of South Africa, selling assorted building materials, chemicals and timber for the Swedish-South Africa Export Import Company. His employer, Albert Floren, wrote a glowing letter about Raoul's organizational skill, "his boundless energy and vitality," his "great imaginative powers" and his "clear and original mind." The other partner in the company, Carl Frykberg, noted that Raoul had the "remarkable gift of quickly and thoroughly acquainting himself with whatever he sets his mind to."

The next step was Haifa. Gustaf felt it was now time for Raoul to get banking experience. He knew a director of the Holland Bank, Erwin Freund, who was willing to take Raoul as a nonpaid employee in the Haifa branch of the bank. He couldn't pay the young man because Raoul could not get a working visa. On his way up from South Africa, Raoul again went to see Gustaf in Nice, and there they had a dispute about Raoul's future. However, he obediently set off for Haifa by boat.

En route, Raoul stopped at Genoa and wrote to his grandfather,

I again want to apologize for losing my temper. I am too conscious of my indebtedness to Grandpa to not go along with your decision. But I am sorry that Grandpa tried to find motives in my objection which I didn't have at all. My intention was strictly to contribute to the plan of the study program which would make it more effective and give it a larger range.

Raoul went on to explain that he had no objection to living abroad, nor any great wish to go home to Stockholm, since "I have neither a job nor money."

No job, no money. That was the inescapable, humiliating truth. Despite the fact that Raoul was a brilliant member of the most powerful family in Sweden, he was in the anomalous position of having to serve as a volunteer in a spot that didn't appeal to him and in which he saw no future.

FOUR

HAIFA, STOCKHOLM AND WAR

Raoul arrived in Haifa just as the Arab uprisings of 1936 were getting under way. Refugees from Hitler's Germany had swelled the Jewish population of British-mandated Palestine. Heavily financed Nazi propaganda had followed them to their new home. The Grand Mufti of Jerusalem, who spent most of the war years in Berlin, was subsidized to fan anti-Semitic flames among Arabs. A young Arab leader, Fawzi al-Qawukji, openly imitated the style of Adolf Hitler, organized military training among Arab nationalists and helped smuggle Axis weapons through Syria and Iraq. The Jews, feeling the British were not affording them protection, began to organize their own defense.

The Arabs were being inflamed by the idea that the British were introducing Jews into Palestine to drive them out. They were stirred up by their leaders with the idea that to the Jews "money is God" and that the Jews would defile holy Jerusalem with their secularism and materialism. Jewish farms were attacked, and a mass work stoppage was called.

Haifa remained relatively free of incidents during the period when Raoul was there, but he wrote afterward in a letter to a friend: "One heard bombings now and then: at least my Jewish friends used to—I suppose their nerves were all gone to pieces, poor people."

Haifa was then a bustling port city. The British had modernized the harbor three years earlier, and refugees had brought the Jewish population up to fifty thousand, triple what it had been five years earlier. There was a housing shortage, and it was customary to share rooms at the pension.

One night Wallenberg came home to find a new roommate— Ariel Kahane. Kahane had been forced to flee Berlin, where he had been trained as an architect, and was looking for work in a land with a most uncertain future. The two young men quickly became involved in talk about architecture. Kahane was overwhelmed when he realized that the young bank clerk, who spoke German like a native and seemed to be "one of us," was actually one of Sweden's elite. Kahane was aware of the Wallenberg name because a member of the family had played a role in the construction of an architecturally noted town hall at Östberg. Raoul showed his companion his plans for the swimming pool in Stockholm as well as plans by another architect for a villa being built by one of his cousins.

In 1980 in Jerusalem, Kahane—by then a retired successful Israeli architect and town planner—recalled his night with Raoul: "We talked late into the night. He was a princeling and I was at the nadir of my career. I was possibly the poorest architect of the time, and he possibly the richest, but we talked on completely equal terms."

Kahane could not possibly have guessed that Raoul's situation was, in its way, as painful as his own. His future was uncertain. And he had no money of his own.

Raoul stuck at his bank job, but it became more and more apparent to him that he was wasting time. In his letter of July 6 he presented the issues to Gustaf fully and clearly:

You can hardly have failed to notice a certain anxiety that has appeared in my letters during the past year. It was based on the fact that, while I thought my present plan of study, which of course is completely your work, certainly was skillfully and logically designed toward the goal that you have set, a foreign bank, it did not very well serve its purpose of preparing me to earn money in the near future. It is true that a couple of years of service at agencies and bank branches as a volunteer abroad gives one, in your view, an appropriate orientation, but that does not qualify one for a well-paid post immediately.

I had a feeling and have it still that it is dangerous to be a volunteer. Merits that you receive have value only if the one who has written a recommendation has been willing himself to pay for you. Besides, I was afraid that the plan was too inflexible. I had a feeling that you were firmly determined that I should stay in Palestine a couple of years no matter what my experiences in the place might be.

This is why I am so pleased with your last letter, for there I see a willingness on your part to fit the plan to the circumstances. On such terms I am willing to cooperate and I can accommodate your wishes more than I had recently thought, for I don't want to conceal the fact that during the past months I had started to think that in order to make myself heard, I would have to cry "wolf" more than was actually called for.

The question is, in other words: Is the Dutch Bank my best opportunity to learn those things that I have to learn? So far it certainly has not been, and I've already said that, but I now notice some improvement. I have now been promised that they will move me to a different department and it's about time because I've been sitting almost three months at the Foreign Exchange engaged in routine work. The staff is too small and the bank was quite simply forced to put me where there wasn't anyone else to step in.

Raoul went on to discuss the possibility of serving in other branches of the Holland Bank, and offered some criticism of the way the bank was conducting its business.

Finally, he came to the crux of the matter. For the first time he expressed the feeling that his temperament was unsuited to the career his grandfather had planned. "Do you think, for example, that if you hadn't had any grandson you would have thought I had the ability to take up your mantle in the future in this special area?" he wrote.

The difficulty of Raoul's "confrontation" was expressed in the closing lines of the letter, in which he acknowledged his debt to his grandfather:

It will much interest me this fall to become acquainted with some of the great men there at home together with you, Grandfather. I can't help

*thinking of the love and care that you have spent on me (not to mention
money), and I see in your trip home further proof of this. If I were a
worthy grandson I would no doubt thank you by following your
direction without questions and objections. Therefore, I have been a bit
ashamed to make the comments and suggestions that I have brought up
now and then, but I do not regret doing it since I don't believe that any
good could come of hiding my apprehensions. As I said, that is why I so
much appreciate your last letter, for it shows a more flexible position in
the question of what I am to do, whether I shall stay here, etc.*

Gustaf didn't quite get the full message. He reassured Raoul:
"Your disappointment at not yet having a real job is not justified: what
you have done up to now has been only to give you experience. I think
that our plan has not failed, because what you have experienced has
surely been of some use." He urges Raoul not to be overly modest and
belittle the praise he has received from his employers.

But Gustaf was still trying to get Raoul a job in a bank.
Interestingly, in writing to his cousin Frederik Wallenberg, he didn't
mention the Enskilda Bank headed by his younger brother Marcus and
Marcus's sons. Perhaps he felt that Raoul would necessarily have to play a
very subordinate role in the Enskilda Bank, living in the shadow of
Marcus's sons, Jacob and Marcus, who were already in charge of major
Wallenberg enterprises. In any case, he appeared to have been bent on
getting Raoul experience outside of the gigantic Wallenberg business,
and far from Stockholm. Totally ignoring Raoul's reference to "unbankish" feelings, Gustaf had been in touch with some of his acquaint-
ances, directors of banks in Bogotá, Calcutta and Bombay, about
securing a position for Raoul that would more effectively prepare him
for a career at the head of an international bank.

In addition to getting Raoul ready for his career, Gustaf told
Frederik he wanted to make a "man" of his grandson, and he said with
pride that Raoul had fulfilled this goal. He spoke of Raoul's skill in
languages, his education in architecture, his broad knowledge of the
world, so far from the Swedish insularity Gustaf disliked. He concluded
the letter by mentioning that Raoul had stopped for a visit with him in
Istanbul. Gustaf said he invited "the cleverest Jew" in the city to lunch
with them. The "clever Jew" had met Raoul when he was a boy taking a
motor trip with Gustaf through Germany. The man had been much
taken with Raoul. Obviously Gustaf wanted to show what a fine man the

bright youngster had become—perhaps he also wanted to see Raoul match wits with the clever man.

Gustaf returned for the visit to Stockholm shortly afterward, but he was not well, and he died on March 21, 1937. His death was mourned in Turkey as well as Sweden. The Turkish obituaries expressed gratitude for his warm friendship with a developing country.

Raoul was now free from Gustaf's dream and was set to make his own way in the world. That proved to be more difficult than might be expected for one who was not only a Wallenberg but a gifted architect, a man with international experience, skill in five languages, charming, distinguished and full of drive.

Raoul's American architectural degree did not qualify him to work in Sweden. He would have had to go back to school to get a Swedish degree, and he had no thought of doing that. He hoped rather to use his knowledge of architecture in some area of business that would involve town planning.

Raoul spoke to his cousin Jacob, the older of the two magnates, about his situation, but nothing was immediately forthcoming.

Raoul decided to go into business for himself, and in 1938 he teamed up with a German refugee who had some patents on industrial products. They set up the Swedish-Swiss Trading Co., and Raoul threw himself into the work with his usual enthusiasm and energy. He traveled to Switzerland and France, where he visited the Paris World Exhibition. While there, he made some trade investigations for Jacob Wallenberg, a job he thoroughly enjoyed.

Unfortunately, the first enterprise didn't work out, and Raoul went into the bottling business with a new partner. This also failed, and Raoul again spoke to his cousin. Jacob evidently recommended him to a business contact, but nothing came of it. On April 27, 1939, Raoul wrote rather desperately to Jacob:

Dear Jacob,

I spoke to President Ljungberg of the Match Company regard ing a position in India. I have unfortunately not received any answer as yet. At a later time I asked him if there was any possibility for another opening somewhere else in the company—to which he answered no. That is depressing. Naturally whatever kind of job it was with a similar salary, I would prefer to work in Europe or America.

It is quite depressing walking around like this waiting, and I would be grateful to you if you would advise me—as you did at the beginning of February—to wait for the job you have in mind for me in the future, or if circumstances are such that you advise me to try to find something on my own. In the first case, I wonder if you have anything I could possibly do in the meantime.

I take this opportunity to thank you warmly for the interest you have shown me and for the steps you have taken in regard to a position for me.

> *Kindly yours,*
> *Raoul Wallenberg*

One can only imagine the pain a letter like that must have cost the proud, ambitious young man. Interestingly, Raoul uses the word *depressing* twice. For a man of Raoul's ambitions and creative energies, the frustration of not getting started on a meaningful career must have been unbearable. Was Jacob harboring some ill feeling toward his young cousin? Unlikely. Raoul's father had been on very friendly terms with his cousins. Jacob kept a maritime painting by Raoul, Sr., on the wall of his home all of his life.

It is possible that Jacob was simply too preoccupied with financial matters of enormous ramifications to take much interest in a struggling young man of "unbankish" temperament. There was something of the dreamer about Raoul. Perhaps he revealed a bit too much of his compassionate nature to his "cool and cynical" cousin. When Raoul returned from Haifa he remained profoundly concerned about the Jews of Nazi Germany. He was in touch with refugees in Sweden and had anonymously provided a small food subsidy for a needy family. His deep personal response to the terrible events abroad was unusual in Sweden at that time.

Raoul was not likely to have struck Jacob as the kind of family member he needed in the Wallenberg enterprises at that moment. Within a few months Jacob was to take over as head of the Swedish trade mission to Nazi Germany. He was to arrange for materials that were to supply the sinews of the Führer's powerful war machine. Jacob's friendship with Goerdeler, who plotted against Hitler, indicates that he was no Nazi, but simply a hardheaded businessman. Sweden planned to take a neutral role in the conflict that was clearly developing. That meant trading profitably with both sides.

Apart from his career frustration, Raoul was happy to be in Stockholm. He enjoyed being close to his family for the first time since he had left for college in 1932. He had a small bachelor apartment close enough to his parents' home to come over for breakfast most mornings. And he had a lively circle of friends, including Gustav von Platen, who later became editor of the Stockholm daily, *Svenska Dagbladet*. He was very much attracted to beautiful young women, but somewhat shy with them. He dated and fell in love with Jeanette von Heidenstam, who was to become Sweden's outstanding woman television personality. He also dated and danced with the beautiful actress Viveca Lindfors on a night she never forgot:

"It was in 1937," she related in New York, on January 17, 1980.

I was only sixteen and I met him at a family party. We danced together and then he invited me up to his grandfather's office—I thought to make love to me. But he spoke to me in an intense voice, very low, almost a whisper, of the terrible things that were being done to the Jews of Germany. I just didn't understand what he was talking about. I thought he was trying to win my sympathy or something. I was just a dumb girl at the time and I had a cold, Swedish soul. I wasn't ready to appreciate a man like that.

Lindfors reports that her attitude at the time was no different from that of other Swedes, who did not like to hear the disturbing vibrations from the turbulent outside world.

"If at that time you asked a Swede what he thought about Nazism or some other important issue, he would probably not know how to respond—and would just get very upset."

The fact is that before the war there was a good deal of pro-Nazi sentiment among some elements of Sweden's upper class and in the military. Sweden had long had strong cultural and business ties with Germany, and Hitler's anti-Semitic policies were not so distasteful as to cause any break in those ties. Germany was regarded as a defense against Russia, with whom Sweden had had uneasy relations since the early nineteenth century. (In 1808 Russia had retaliated for a Swedish attack by taking Finland from Sweden's domination.) During World War I considerable pressure was exerted on Sweden to join Germany and attack czarist Russia. However, K.A. Wallenberg (Raoul's granduncle) as foreign minister and Hjalmar Hammarskjöld as prime minister stood firm for neutrality. The result was that Sweden avoided a devastating war, traded with the warring nations, and emerged economically stronger.

She became a strong advocate of international law and order and an ardent supporter of the League of Nations.

The gathering storm in Europe affected Sweden in the mid-thirties, when Jewish refugees from Nazi Germany began clamoring at the gates. Sweden had long had a law permitting aliens to remain in the country for three months without a visa, but in the face of this clamor the regulation was revoked. There was little moral sensitivity to the Nazi atrocities against the Jews. At this period Sweden was suffering from widespread unemployment as a result of the international economic depression, and both business and the general public began to fear a "Jewish invasion." When Stockholm University wanted to invite nine eminent Jewish professors from Germany, the medical students demonstrated against it. Up to the beginning of the war a total of about three thousand refugees were admitted from Germany, Austria and Czechoslovakia. After Kristallnacht, November 9, 1938, when the Nazis burned synagogues all over the country and had an anti-Semitic orgy in the streets of Berlin, Sweden granted entry permits to 150 adults and 500 children. The 8,000 Jews of Sweden were uneasy and maintained a low profile on the issue of immigration. They had enjoyed freedom from persecution in Sweden and were fearful that an influx of refugees would rouse latent anti-Semitism.

It should be noted that Swedish attitudes and policies were far from unique. Most countries of the world had doctrinaire Nazis and Nazi sympathizers. They were decidedly in the minority, but there was enough traditional anti-Semitism in the world, some open and some merely unexpressed, to make the matter of persecuted Jews an uncomfortable issue. While most people would not like to be responsible for exterminating Jews, there was some validity to Hitler and Goebbels' often-stated belief that Anglo-American criticism of the Third Reich's anti-Semitic policies was sheer hypocrisy—that secretly the world was pleased that Germany was finding a "solution" to the "Jewish problem." The "problem" appeared to be that Jews existed.

Certainly, the Jews had sympathizers, but not very many were willing or able to do something substantial to help them. And the Jews themselves in every country, including the United States, were uneasy about pressing the issue—particularly in view of the alarming rise of a Nazi movement in the United States in the late thirties. There was not only the German-American Bund; home-grown anti-Semitic groups were surfacing. The early reaction of the mass of American Jews, before they learned about Hitler's extermination plans, was fear for what could happen at home. On the other hand, they viewed as alarmist the predictions of Zionist Revisionist leader Vladimir Jabotinsky (Menachem Begin's mentor) that unless the Jews were evacuated from Europe, they would be destroyed.

The world's essential indifference was brought home with resounding impact at an international conference held at Evian in 1938. President Roosevelt, urged by his Jewish constituency, called the conference to deal with "the refugee problem." But after a good deal of discussion one fact emerged: No country in the world was ready to offer a substantial resettlement program except the Dominican Republic. Later suggestions for Jewish resettlement in Tanganyika, British Guiana, Madagascar and Ethiopia fell through.

On the eve of the war shiploads of refugees in unseaworthy craft sailed the seas and were turned away at every port. For example, the S.S. *St. Louis,* an elegant transatlantic liner with 930 mainly upper-middle-class refugees holding landing permits for Havana, was refused admission there. The Cuban government had invalidated the permits a week earlier, but failed to notify the passengers. The ship hovered in the coastal waters off Florida for weeks while American Jewish leaders tried to get the Immigration Department to admit the refugees. (The quota for the year had not yet been filled.) However, they had no success and the captain was forced to turn the ship back and recross the Atlantic. The passengers were distributed among Britain, France, Holland and Belgium. Only a small percentage survived the war.

On September 2, 1939, the day before the outbreak of World War II, the British fired at *Tiger Hill*, a ship carrying 1,400 "illegal immigrants" to Palestine. Immigration to the Holy Land was severely limited, despite the crisis situation, by a White Paper issued by the British on May 17, 1939, a document strongly opposed by many British political leaders, including Winston Churchill.

If Hitler got the message that as far as the world was concerned he was free to do as he wished about the Jews, he was not altogether irrational. Of course, the world could not yet envision the savagery of the Final Solution.

When the war broke out, Sweden immediately embarked on the neutrality policy that had worked so successfully in World War I.

Marcus and Jacob Wallenberg were chosen to head the vitally important trade missions to Great Britain and Germany respectively.

Marcus Wallenberg was first dispatched to London, along with Secretary-General for Foreign Affairs Erik Boheman. Britain's objective was to monopolize iron ore in order to prevent Germany from getting it. From a Swedish point of view, Britain's demands had to be held down because the German needs had to be satisfied. Sweden promised to keep the iron ore exports to Germany at 1938 levels—eight million tons. This was an unwritten agreement. The British counted on preventing some of the exports from reaching Germany when the carriers moved south from Narvik, outside of Norwegian territorial waters. (The British were satisfied with the agreement, which was concluded in mid-December.)

Then Jacob Wallenberg joined the Swedish minister in Berlin, Arvid Richert, in trade negotiations with Germany. Sweden's goals in relation to Germany were, first, to get more imports, particularly of coke and coal, because it was expected that these would no longer be available from the West; and second, to get the Germans to be more polite in their sea warfare. Swedish ships were being sunk on their way to England, and those bound for Holland, Belgium and the United States were being detained for contraband inspection.

Sweden wound up granting Germany ten million tons of iron ore for 1940 without technically breaking the agreement with Great Britain. It was done in this way: Normally two million tons of ore would have gone to Poland and Czechoslovakia, but Germany was now in control of both those countries. Therefore, Germany had to get the additional resources plus the immense quantities of ball bearings vital to her war machine. Sweden was well satisfied with the work of the Wallenberg brothers.

Throughout the war Marcus Wallenberg maintained close ties with Great Britain and Jacob with Germany. However, after the failed assassination attempt on Hitler on July 20, 1944, in which Jacob's friend Goerdeler was involved, Jacob was warned to stay out of Germany. Up to that point it would appear that if any separate peace between Germany and the West was being contemplated, the Wallenberg brothers would have been natural conduits of information and would be involved in negotiations. Nevertheless, at the same time, Marcus Wallenberg maintained friendly relations with Mme. Alexandra Kollontay, the Russian ambassador in Stockholm. At one point in 1944, in response to her request, he went to Finland to try to talk the Finns into coming to terms with the Soviet Union.

(Marcus commented on his and his brother's wartime roles in *Euromoney*, October 1980: *I used to say that the definition of being neutral—often called bloody neutral—is that you are bawled out by everybody, by all sides. We fulfilled that very well. We were bawled out by everyone. I know that the different camps always thought that we were doing something more favorable to the other camp, but that was not the policy. We had to make restrictions. You [first the British, then the British and Americans] were blockading us. We had to negotiate to get through with this blockade. I was out there arguing our case.)*

The fact is that the trade agreements with the West were gravely hampered because the Germans immediately mined the waters off Falsterbo, at the southern tip of Sweden, as well as the territorial waters off Norway. The British attempted, less successfully, to blockade the Germans, and began an active smuggling trade. Following the German invasion of Norway in April, 1940, the British captured Narvik in northern Norway and the Germans had to retreat to Norway's Swedish border. The Germans then pressed the Swedes to allow troop transit through their country. Sweden resisted, then agreed to permit passage only for medical supplies and transport of troops for purposes of leave. It soon became apparent that more troops were going to Norway than coming out on leave, and that weapons were being brought into Norway in the guise of Red Cross transport.

Germany had occupied Norway, Denmark, Luxembourg and Belgium by the spring of 1940. The Soviet Union took advantage of its nonaggression pact with Germany to move into Finland and the Baltic states—Estonia, Lithuania and Latvia, across the sea from Sweden. Sweden was surrounded by occupied countries. The Germans kept increasing their demands for transit privileges. When the Swedes resisted, the Germans made threatening noises. The Western Allies wanted to come to Sweden's aid, but the nation's political leaders were convinced that any gesture in that direction would lead to immediate occupation by the Germans. Finally, in 1941 Sweden permitted a fully equipped German division to travel through from Norway to Finland. However, the Finns welcomed German help in routing the Russians.

While the Swedish government saw no alternative to compliance with German demands, the Swedish public became increasingly hostile toward Nazism and sympathetic toward its victims. When Norway's quisling government set out to deport and hand over to the Germans the country's seventeen hundred Jews in November 1942, Swedes as individuals cooperated with Norwegian sympathizers of Jews. Together they managed to smuggle more than eight hundred across the border into Sweden. The other half of Norway's Jews were deported to Auschwitz; twenty-five of them survived the war.

In October 1943 Sweden gave asylum to nearly eight thousand of Denmark's Jews and half Jews, and Gentiles married to Jews, in the most dramatic rescue operation of the Holocaust. The entire Danish population cooperated in hiding Jews and transporting them on a dangerous journey across the blockaded seaways to Sweden.

Neutral Sweden seemed remote from the war to Europeans suffering its ravages, but the nation fully experienced the war's shock waves. Far from standing apart from the fray, Stockholm became one of the main centers in Europe for the exchange of information, along with Geneva and Istanbul. Couriers, spies and counterspies were actively giving and receiving information in Stockholm. The Swedish Foreign Office was among the first to get substantial and sensational firsthand knowledge of the Final Solution.

The first information came from the "Warsaw Swedes," a Swedish colony in Warsaw with sympathy for both the Poles and Jews. One of these Swedes, Sven Norrman, went into the Warsaw ghetto and shot film of the atrocities going on there. Norrman, head of ASEA, an electro-technical corporation connected with the Wallenberg interests, and Carl Wilhelm Herslow, Warsaw director of the Polish safety-match state monopoly which was part of the old Swedish Ivar Kreuger concern, would frequently visit Stockholm and report to the Swedish Foreign Office and King Gustaf V.

The second source involved one of the most extraordinary incidents of World War II. The information was delivered in the crowded corridor of the Warsaw–Berlin express train in August 1942 by Kurt Gerstein, chief "disinfection" officer of the SS, to Swedish diplomat Baron von Otter. Gerstein had helped develop and deliver the Zyklon-B gas that was to be used in the extermination centers.

Gerstein claimed he joined the SS with the plan of learning what was going on inside the inner circle in Nazi Germany. A relative of his had suddenly mysteriously died in a mental institution. When he did some detective work he learned of the Nazis' early secret euthanasia projects, intended to purify the Aryan race through killing off the mentally retarded and mentally ill.

Gerstein told von Otter he had just come from a "corpse factory" known as Belzec in eastern Poland. He reported the killings of thousands at a time by gas. He had seen collections of gold teeth pulled out of the mouths of corpses. One especially horrifying event he witnessed was a mass killing at which something had gone wrong with the gas-release mechanism. He had timed the death agony of the jammed-together bodies with a stopwatch. It had taken over three hours. There were many corpse factories like this in East Europe.

Gerstein showed his identification documents to von Otter and told him to get the information out to the world. He believed the German people would rise against Nazism if they knew what was going on.

In his book, *The Terrible Secret*, historian Walter Laqueur claims that von Otter passed the information on to Staffan Söderblom, then head of the political department of the Swedish Foreign Ministry. He buried it in the files because "We judged it too risky to pass information from one belligerent country to another." (The cautious Mr. Söderblom, later Sweden's ambassador to Moscow, was to play an important role in blocking the investigation into Wallenberg's disappearance, in the interest of protecting the Soviet's image and preserving Sweden's good relations with them.)

It is possible that Raoul Wallenberg's efforts to rescue Jews would have begun earlier if the Gerstein story had been told to the world. However, action would require political power, and he was involved with no political group.

In the view of Raoul's half-sister, Mrs. Nina Lagergren, "Raoul just wasn't a political person—he did what he did out of his feelings. He hated stupid bullies and pompous people and he hated seeing people pushed around."

During this period Raoul lived the life of an upper-class Swedish citizen. He enjoyed social life, but he also became deeply involved in Finnish War Relief during the Winter War of 1939–40 when the Finns put up stiff resistance against the Soviet forces. He served in the Home Guard and became an outstanding officer who on weekends led his company on strenuous jaunts and maneuvers in the countryside outside of Stockholm.

Nina got a hint of where Raoul's feelings were taking him when she went to see a film with him during the winter of 1942. It was called *Pimpernel Smith*, a takeoff on the Baroness Orczy novel, *The Scarlet Pimpernel*, about an imaginative hero who saved aristocrats during the French Revolution through ingenious ruses. In the American film an absentminded professor, played by Leslie Howard, manages to save Jews from the Nazis. The sister and brother both took great delight in the movie, and when it was over Raoul confided in Nina that he'd like to emulate the professor. She took it as a passing fancy. But Raoul was by that time profoundly concerned. The catastrophic events in Europe had been brought home to him in a very direct way.

FIVE

PREPARA-TION FOR A MISSION

The night Raoul and Nina saw *Pimpernel Smith* together, Raoul was already on the path toward his mission in Budapest, but he didn't know it. The mission came about as a direct result of his association with Koloman Lauer, a Hungarian Jew Raoul had met in the fall of 1941 through his cousin Jacob. Lauer was head of the largest food-trading enterprise in central Europe, Meropa AB. He had emigrated with his family to Sweden before the war broke out. In the past he had traveled throughout Europe, buying food for packaging, canning and selling to distributors. With the Nazis in control of most of Europe, he was no longer able to travel freely.

Lauer immediately liked the eager, energetic young man. Raoul's international background, his facility in French, German and English, his ability to relate to all kinds of people and his business experience made him an ideal representative for the company. Raoul was taken on as a junior partner, and although Lauer was considerably older than Raoul, the business relationship developed into friendship.

Raoul spent his first few months getting acquainted with the business in Stockholm. By Christmas of 1941 he was ready to take on his role as trade representative. He left for France. He went first to Vichy, the capital of the so-called Free Zone, which was actually entirely under the domination of the Nazi military organization.

The Free Zone comprised two thirds of France and was an important food-producing center. Some of the businessmen Wallenberg contacted there were undoubtedly Jews who were still trying to function under severely restrictive laws and were threatened by factors they couldn't predict. The small, centuries-old Jewish communities of the region were left unmolested, but there was the smell of fear in the atmosphere. The French Jews saw many of their countrymen collaborate with France's traditional enemies, the Germans; they were suddenly united by a common anti-Semitism.

The Germans had already deported some 76,000 Jews from Alsace-Lorraine into Vichy, along with "asocials," criminals, Gypsies and insane people. In addition, they had dumped 7,450 Jews from Germany's Baden-Saar into the area. These, along with thousands of refugees who had fled Germany, Austria, Poland, Holland and Belgium, were thrown into twenty-six primitive internment camps maintained by sadistic French guards. The death rate from starvation, cold, disease and abuse was extremely high. A nonsectarian group in the region, the Nimes Committee, tried to alleviate conditions in the camps and managed to help some prisoners escape. The survivors were eventually deported to Auschwitz.

After about a week in Vichy, Wallenberg moved on to Paris, where he spent the first twenty-eight days of January 1942. Paris was a sad city, with most of the French gritting their teeth at the sight of the Germans arrogantly disporting themselves. Of course, even Paris had its home-grown Nazi sympathizers who made the Germans feel very much at home. Wallenberg, as the representative of a well-known Jewish businessman, met some of the leading business people of the city. About 200,000 of France's 270,000 Jews lived in Paris—and they were suffering severely.

Adolf Eichmann's IV B4 office, concerned with the rooting out of Jews and Jewish life, had been functioning in Paris for more than a year and a half. The office was led by SS *Hauptsturmführer* Theodor Dannecker (who Wallenberg would encounter two years later in Budapest). Dannecker was making a street-to-street survey of the

Parisian Jews. As a result of this survey 3,649 naturalized Polish Jews had already been rounded up and were interned in camps. In August there had been another seizure of 3,429 Jews involved in what the Nazis called "Communist de Gaullist misdeeds and assassination attempts against members of the *Wehrmacht*." These too were interned and eventually were deported, mainly to Auschwitz.

In addition, Jewish enterprises had to be declared as such, and proceeds from the forced sale of Jewish property were blocked. A fine of a billion francs had been imposed on the Jewish community. There had been a bungled attempt to blow up two synagogues. The Germans had ordered the creation of an organization known as the *Union Générale des Israélites de France*, which was destined to be the French counterpart of the Polish *Judenrat* (Jewish Councils). The Germans set it up to serve as their administrative instrument, for carrying out their orders. However, this organization had many units, and some of the units were actually working on the creation of a rescue apparatus. At this time the young French Zionists and the French-Jewish scout organization were preparing to play an active role in the rescue and hiding of children and families in southern France.

The Jews of Paris were not yet required to wear the yellow star, but this was to come the following month.

Wallenberg had many important matters to transact in order to keep international business lines open during wartime. This threw him into contact with a variety of people. As a Wallenberg, a "neutral" Swede, a businessman who spoke excellent French and perfect German, he had access to three worlds—the Jewish, the French-gentile and the Nazi occupiers. He could not have left France without a good understanding of what German occupation entailed and how Jews and their compatriots responded to it.

At the end of January Wallenberg returned to Stockholm via Zurich, and a week later he set out for Budapest, where he remained for several weeks. The atmosphere in Budapest was very different from the despair and shame he had encountered in Paris. Budapest was called the Paris of East Europe, and at that time it was the *only* Paris, still sparkling with theater and café life and people who seemed to feel strangely isolated from the war raging around them.

Hungary was an anomaly and a paradox. Although it was an Axis power, it had become a haven for refugees fleeing from Poland, Austria and Germany. Three major pieces of anti-Jewish legislation had been passed in the country. Two massacres had taken place. In one some eighteen thousand "alien" Jews, from territories regained by Hungary as a reward for her alliance with Hitler, had been deported and killed near Kamenets-Podolsk on Soviet soil. The other had taken place in late January, just before Wallenberg's arrival. More than three thousand partisans and Jews from Délvidék, the Hungarian-occupied portion of Yugoslavia, had been massacred after sadistic abuses.

The Budapest Jews had gotten firsthand accounts of these horrors. Moreover, they also knew from German and Polish refugees what the Nazis were capable of doing. Yet they had a false sense of security. A large proportion of them were so assimilated into Hungarian life and culture that they couldn't believe they could be put in the same category with "Eastern Jews." The country's regent, Miklós Horthy, was no lover of Jews ("I have been an anti-Semite all my life!" he once retorted to pro-Nazi critics, proudly pointing to the fact that Hungary had been first in post-World War I Europe to institute anti-Jewish legislation), but he was a realist. He felt the country needed Jews to keep the wheels of business and industry turning. At the time Wallenberg arrived, Horthy was planning to get rid of his strongly pro-German prime minister, László Bárdossy, and replace him with the more moderate Miklós Kállay.

The Jewish business people Wallenberg encountered on this trip to Budapest were among the group who felt that there was little choice except to be optimistic and trust that the liberal forces, which still had some leverage in the Hungarian Parliament, would be able to control the Nazi fanatics. A good many Budapest Jews had family ties with Christians and with Hungarian aristocracy. They had lived with anti-Semitism for a long time and believed there were ways of getting around it and surviving.

Wallenberg was not likely to meet at this time those Jews working frantically in the Jewish underground, urging courageous young men and women to accept money and false papers and flee for their lives through escape routes the Zionists had set up via Bucharest and Istanbul.

Before returning to Stockholm Wallenberg made brief stops in Switzerland and Berlin, gaining firsthand knowledge about what was going on in Europe. By inclination and training he was an information gatherer and an analyst of social and economic conditions. These qualities made him an excellent trade representative. His old talent for debating emerged. He had endless persistence and patience, learning to understand his client's point of view and generally managing to come out with a deal satisfactory to both sides. Because his work entailed intricate trade and monetary negotiations, he developed some expertise in dealing with Nazi red tape. All of this experience was soon to stand him in good stead.

While Wallenberg was pursuing his life as a businessman, his destiny was being shaped by factors very remote from him.

On January 20, 1942, a high-level Nazi conference was held in Wannsee, a Berlin suburb. Reinhard Heydrich, who had been charged by Hitler with the job of bringing about "a complete solution of the Jewish question in the German sphere of influence in Europe," had called together a conference of undersecretaries of state, police and SS officials to outline the details of the Final Solution.

The project for exterminating the Jews had actually been in effect for nearly a year. Well over a million had already been killed by the *Einsatzgruppen*, special machine-gunning squads which accompanied Nazi troops in their sweep into Russia, and by local pogroms all over Poland. Effective means for the murder of many more millions had not yet been developed, but experiments with a new gas were promising. With the new gas, thousands could be killed at one time.

Heydrich outlined the general plan that was to be followed. Jews must first be identified and isolated, then evacuated and put to forced labor in the East. He expected that most would die off under the conditions to which they would be subjected. The survivors would have to be "treated accordingly," a code word for killed.

This was to be the fate of all the Jews of Europe, including those in as-yet-unconquered areas—England, Ireland, Spain, Sweden.

When Eichmann, who was present at the Wannsee conference, described the occasion in 1953 in an interview with a Dutch journalist in Argentina (published in *Life* Magazine November 28 and December 5, 1960), he recalled nostalgically that after their hard day of absorbing all that Heydrich told them, the group sat around singing and drinking.

After a while we got up on the chairs and drank a toast, then on the table and then round and round—on the chairs and on the table again. Heydrich taught it to us. It was an old North German custom. But we sat around peacefully after our Wannsee Conference, not just talking shop, but giving ourselves a rest after so many taxing hours.

In mid-1942 the existence of a plan for the systematic extermination of the Jews of Europe was both known and not known by the world. There had been published reports about atrocities and massacres, but these were generally viewed as isolated events taking place within the context of a fierce war and probably much exaggerated by "Jewish hysteria." The reports were too terrible to be believed.

However, by the end of 1942, world leaders had more facts than they were ready to acknowledge. Each power had different reasons for the suppression of information:

1. The Soviet Union had experienced the massacre of more than a million Jewish citizens during the Nazi drive toward Moscow, but the government had never publicized the fact that most of the slaughtered "peaceful citizens," as described in Russian dispatches, were Jews, and that the Nazis had a special hatred of Jews. Stalin's own deep-rooted anti-Semitism would not permit him to risk the possibility that any sympathy might arise for Jews. The secret of Nazi anti-Semitism had been so well kept that when the Germans marched into Russia they were greeted in many areas with flowers as "liberators" by Jews who had suffered severely under the Soviet regime.

2. The British feared intensification of pressures on the government to admit more Jews to Palestine. They were determined to stick to the decision pronounced in the White Paper of 1939, restricting Jewish immigration to seventy-five thousand over five years. They admitted 50,000 refugees to Great Britain, but feared a Jewish exodus to Palestine.

3. In the United States, the State Department was in charge of the "refugee problem." The department was dominated by individuals actively unsympathetic to Jews.

Late in 1942 the American State Department and the British Foreign Office were forced to acknowledge that the Nazis were serious about killing off all the Jews of Europe, and that they had the technical means to accomplish their objective. The news had been working its way through channels for nearly six months. At that point a groundswell of public protest built up in Britain and the United States. A new international conference on refugees was set for April 19, 1943, in Bermuda. By that time three million Jews were already dead.

Virtually nothing was accomplished in Bermuda. Neither the United States nor Britain had any intention of changing its policies on refugees. The rationalization given was that any rescue program for the Jews might impede the war effort. No negotiations with Germany were possible. No shipping for refugees was available. No funds were available. No relief supplies could be sent to the death camps.

While the Bermuda Conference was going on, the Jews in the Warsaw ghetto were fighting the Germans with an assortment of hand grenades, homemade explosives, and seven Polish rifles, one Soviet rifle, one German rifle and fifty-nine pistols. They received no help from the Polish population outside the walls. On May 12, 1943, two weeks after the Bermuda Conference ended, forty-eight-year-old Szmul Zygielbojm, a member of the Polish National Council in London and a Jewish labor leader, committed suicide, leaving a note saying, "By my death I wish to make my final protest against the passivity with which the world is looking on and permitting the extermination of the Jewish people." *The New York Times* published his letter in an inconspicuous spot in the paper.

Despite continuing public clamor, World War II might have ended without any decisive official effort to save the remaining Jews of Europe, and without Wallenberg's rescue mission to Budapest, if it had not been for a serious disagreement in the Roosevelt administration. Henry Morgenthau, Jr., secretary of the treasury, shared with the State Department certain responsibilities relating to refugee issues. Two young men in his department—General Counsel Josiah E. DuBois, Jr., and head of the Foreign Fund Control Division John Pehle, Jr.,—became aware that the State Department was suppressing information about an opportunity to ransom thousands of refugees from Romanian prison camps in Transnistria, a barren waste in the Ukraine. With the approval of Morgenthau they prepared a memorandum on bungling and suppression of information about refugee issues within the State Department. This was presented to President Roosevelt.

A struggle within the administration ensued. It was finally resolved by a decision to set up a special agency to help "rescue the victims of enemy oppression who are in imminent danger of death." The agency was to have powers to attempt to block "Nazi plans to exterminate all the Jews."

The problem was at last squarely confronted, but the date was January 1944, a time when only one large Jewish community remained in Europe—that of Hungary. The rescue agency, the War Refugee Board, was established on January 22, and it was presented with a major challenge eight weeks later. Germany occupied Hungary, its former ally, on March 19, and Adolf Eichmann was immediately dispatched to Budapest to implement "the solution to the Jewish problem."

Pehle, appointed director of the new agency, immediately went into action. He appealed to the neutral powers, the International Red Cross and the Vatican to take measures to save Hungarian Jewry. President Roosevelt issued an appeal to the Hungarian people to help the Jews, and a warning that those who participated in crimes against them would be punished as war criminals. British Foreign Minister Anthony Eden followed with a similar message.

There was no stampede in Hungary to aid Hungarian Jewry. On the contrary, with rare exceptions the Hungarian authorities participated enthusiastically in Eichmann's deportation program. The International Red Cross stood by its position that these matters were "beyond our capabilities." The Catholic Primate of Hungary pleaded for a distinction between baptized Jews and the others. He had some success—the baptized Jews were permitted to wear a white cross along with the yellow star that was required of all other Jews. There was no immediate response from the neutral nations.

Eichmann's death machinery moved swiftly and smoothly. Jews were required to wear their yellow stars, then they were ghettoized in preparation for "deportation," and on May 5 the packed cattle cars started moving, carrying ten thousand to twelve thousand a day to Auschwitz and other death camps. The facilities at Auschwitz had been prepared for an overload, and the crematoria went on a round-the-clock schedule.

Iver C. Olsen, a Treasury Department functionary with connections to the Office of Strategic Services (OSS), wartime predecessor of the CIA, was sent to Stockholm by the War Refugee Board to try to stir some action, possibly to send an official representative of neutral Sweden to Budapest to intervene for the remaining Jews. He was told that one hundred thousand dollars would be available from the WRB and at least as much from the American Jewish Joint Distribution Committee for a rescue program.

Olsen talked things over with leaders of the Jewish community in Stockholm, and plans were discussed for getting Jews out of Hungary. The Swedish Jews were in a painful position—they wanted to help, but were frightened that an influx of Jews would rearouse the anti-Semitism that had flared only a few years earlier.

At the same time Koloman Lauer was in an agony of worry about his wife's family in Hungary. Wallenberg was eager to go to Budapest to try to help them, but his request for a visa had been turned down. When Lauer learned that Olsen was interested in finding someone who could be sent on a diplomatic mission, he immediately recommended his young partner.

Olsen met with Wallenberg on June 9. By that time tens of thousands of Hungarian Jews had already gone up in smoke and the remainder were awaiting their turn. Olsen was enormously impressed with the young man, and was convinced he had found the right combination of dedication and skill for the rescue mission. Rabbi Marcus Ehrenpreis, the chief rabbi of Stockholm, was dubious. Wallenberg seemed so young, so unlike the imposing personages who were normally sent on diplomatic missions. However, after a lengthy interview with Wallenberg, he too was impressed. Herschel V. Johnson, American ambassador to Sweden, also approved the choice. He reported to the secretary of state that Wallenberg was half Jewish. Wallenberg evidently felt that a reference to his Jewish great-great-grandfather would enhance his qualifications for the job. In the same communication Johnson states that the Hungarian Jews, "in spite of all their difficulties have collected money to the equivalent of two million Swedish crowns (about five hundred thousand dollars) and this has been turned over to the Swedish Legation in Budapest."

Wallenberg made a strong point of the fact that he would undertake the mission only if he was given freedom from the normal restrictions imposed upon diplomats. He obviously had a realistic picture both of diplomatic procedures and of the job he was facing when he enumerated the following conditions:

1. He would be free to use any methods he chose, including bribery.

2. He should be free to return to Stockholm for consultations with the foreign office without having to get permission.

3. If his funds ran out, a money-raising campaign would be conducted in Sweden.

4. He should be given the title of first secretary of the legation at a salary of two thousand crowns (five hundred dollars) a month.

5. He should be free to have contacts with anyone he chose, including the enemy of the official government.

6. He should have the power to deal directly with any members of the Hungarian government he chose without going through the ambassador.

7. He should have the privilege of sending dispatches to Stockholm via the diplomatic courier.

8. He should have the right to request an interview with Regent Horthy to ask for his help.

9. He should be permitted to give asylum in Swedish legation buildings to individuals under Swedish protection.

There must have been surprise in the foreign office at these brash stipulations from a thirty-one-year-old who had never been processed in its bureaucratic machinery. Yet the terms were approved. Could it have been because the Swedish government felt that it had a good deal to make up for in view of its services to Nazi Germany throughout the war? Did the fact that the Allies made a successful landing in Normandy on June 6, and the war had taken a decisive turn against Germany, have something to do with the foreign office's decision? Perhaps both factors influenced diplomatic thinking; in any case, Wallenberg got his appointment, which came through on June 23.

(The Swedish king later received an extraordinary letter, dated June 27, apparently smuggled out of Budapest, hand-written in French on graph paper torn from a notebook and signed by "The Bureau in Charge of the Jews of Hungary." [No agency of that name existed.] The author or authors pitifully implored the King to send to Budapest *"immediately*, in the last minute of the last hour," Count Folke Bernadotte, vice-chairman of the Swedish Red Cross, to rescue the people of Budapest who were "condemned to the most terrible death." The senders of the letter obviously felt that nobody of less importance than Bernadotte would be able to intercede. Bernadotte had been considered, but the decision was finally made to send Wallenberg.)

At the time the appointment was made, Wallenberg planned to leave for Budapest at the beginning of August. This is a clear indication that the horrifying situation in Hungary was still not understood or believed. Adolf Eichmann, one of Hitler's chief technicians of slaughter, was transporting ten thousand to twelve thousand Jews a day to the gas chambers. The countryside was virtually *judenrein* (free of Jews) already.

When Wallenberg sat down to study the reports that were coming in he realized this and immediately changed his plans. He would leave as soon as possible, but he needed briefing on the Hungarian political situation.

Wallenberg had excellent sources of information in Stockholm. First, there was Wilmos Böhm, formerly a prominent Hungarian leftist leader and journalist. He had been living in exile in Sweden and was employed by the British legation as a reader and analyst of news from Hungary. He was able to supply Wallenberg with the names of political figures who might be helpful and with a picture of general conditions in Hungary. Lauer offered the names of business people and political and professional figures. The Jewish community had its own sources of information. Rabbi Ehrenpreis kept in touch with Dr. Zwi Taubes, the chief rabbi of Zurich. Hillel Storch, representative for the World Jewish Congress and the Jewish Agency Rescue Committee, was aware of individuals involved in rescue operations all over Europe. Norbert Masur and Fritz Hollander, businessmen active in the World Jewish Congress, also had contacts in Hungary and other parts of Europe.

While Wallenberg was making his preparations, the first full, detailed report about the Auschwitz death camp reached Stockholm. Five Jews had escaped separately from Auschwitz. Two of them, Walter Rosenberg (Rudolf Vrba) and Alfred Wetzler (Josef Lanik), had jobs in the camp that enabled them to move about and observe the total operation. They made their way on foot through Poland and reached the Slovakian border on April 21. There they related the full story of how prisoners lived and died in the camp. They described where the various buildings, including the crematoria, were located. A member of the Jewish Council, Oskar (Karmil) Krasznyansky, added to the report architects' sketches of the Auschwitz camp setup and biographical data on the sources of information. He vouched for their authenticity, and added a supplement urging the Allies to bomb the crematoria and the railroad lines leading to Auschwitz.

Copies of the report, known as the "Auschwitz Protocols," were forwarded to Istanbul, Geneva, the Papal Nuncio in Bratislava and to Rudolf Kasztner, Zionist leader in Budapest, at the end of April.

During the last week of June reports about the incredible brutality of the deportations from Budapest reached Stockholm. They told of how Jews were crammed eighty to a cattle car, containing two buckets, one filled with water and one for waste, and shipped for a four-day journey to Auschwitz and other death camps.

On July 1 Ambassador Johnson sent Secretary of State Cordell Hull a cable which stated that his information from Budapest was so terrible "that it is hard to believe and there are no words to qualify its description." He said that of over 600,000 Jews in Hungary, there were now fewer than 400,000. (His figures were confused: A closer approximation is that there were 800,000 Jews in Hungary, with about 200,000 in Budapest when the Germans occupied the country. Close to 450,000 had been deported when he wrote his report.)

These reports had their impact. Strongly worded protests were sent to Regent Horthy on June 25 from the Pope, on June 26 from President Roosevelt, on June 30 from King Gustav V. The suggestion to bomb the crematoria and rail lines to Auschwitz was turned down on June 26 by the War Department as being "impracticable." John Pehle, the WRB director, evidently unaware that the request had already been turned down, put through his own report and a new request for bombing to Assistant Secretary of War John J. McCloy on June 29. The clock was ticking for hundreds of thousands still alive in Auschwitz or on their way to the camp.

Wallenberg set July 6 for his departure date. The night before he left he got together with the leaders of the Jewish community in Stockholm, including Rabbi Ehrenpreis, who blessed him. Among those present was a businessman, Fritz Hollander.

"It was a very solemn evening," recalled Hollander in June 1980. "We knew what had already happened and we knew he was going on a dangerous mission. But we had one thought—that his name would be a protection; the Germans wouldn't dare to harm a Wallenberg. We had no thought at all about the Russians."

Hollander and Lauer drove Wallenberg to the airport the following morning. He was going via Berlin because he wanted to stop for a visit with his sister Nina. She was by that time married to Gunnar Lagergren, an attaché with the Swedish Embassy in Berlin, and she was pregnant with their first child.

Wallenberg stayed overnight with the Lagergrens, talking half the night and then going down to an air-raid shelter with them.

"We saw these Christmas trees, as we called them, lighted triangles that they would send down before a raid to illuminate the area they were going to bomb," Nina Lagergren recalls. "It looked as if it would be a big raid, so we decided to take shelter." Wallenberg was more worried about his sister than she about him. There were daily raids over Berlin, whereas Budapest had experienced only spasmodic raids. Nina realized Raoul's mission was dangerous, but she could not imagine how dangerous it was to become.

Arrangements had been made for Wallenberg to leave by train for Budapest on July 9. He was very much annoyed and said he would not wait—every day counted.

The next day he left on a train crowded with German troops. He couldn't get a seat, so he sat on his rucksack and sleeping bag in the corridor on the slow overnight trip. The train was halted many times during the journey because of war conditions.

In his pocket Wallenberg carried the names of forty important contacts in Budapest. He wore what was called at the time an Anthony Eden hat, a homburg named for the British diplomat, and a long trench coat and he carried a revolver.

SIX

EICHMANN IN BUDAPEST

As Raoul Wallenberg's train rolled southeast from Berlin toward Budapest, the last of eight freight trains bearing the Jews of the suburbs of Budapest and the towns around the capital was rolling north toward Auschwitz. The official count of deported Jews between May 15 and July 8 was 434,351, according to Lieutenant Colonel László Ferenczy, commander of the Hungarian gendarmerie, which executed the entire operation under the supervision of German SS officers. Reich plenipotentiary in Budapest Edmund Veesenmayer reported 437,402 three days later. It is possible that the gendarmes had forgotten to include the Jews from one of the deportation centers.

Nearly all the deportees were sent to Auschwitz, where Dr. Josef Mengele, the camp's notorious medical experimenter, stood at the arrival site to make on-the-spot selections of those fit for labor. Many of the ill and elderly died in the sealed cars during the four-day journey through the countryside in the early summer heat. The Hungarians who stepped out of the cars were mainly women, children and older people, since a large percentage of the young men were serving in Hungarian forced-labor service companies. They arrived exhausted, dazed and dehydrated, thinking only about the water and "showers" they were told

67

they were being led to. Dr. Mengele found only 10 percent fit for labor. The others were sent directly to the gassing chambers.

The entire process of sorting and assembling the Jews and stripping them of property before the entrainment was executed by the Hungarian gendarmes with so much sadistic zeal that the German Nazi supervisors were inspired to make films of the operation. The films were later shown to world press representatives in Switzerland to prove that local populations, not Germans, were responsible for the reported atrocities against the Jews. They showed contrasting films of German soldiers being kind and helpful to Jews arriving at the end of their journey.

Despite the enthusiasm of Hungarian Nazis for the task of dejewifying their country, full murderous credit must be given to Adolf Eichmann for the dedication, drive and organizational skill he brought to his task in Hungary.

A myth has developed that Eichmann was the arch bureaucrat, a man who was just "doing my job" with no interest in the consequences or moral implications of what he was doing. Political philosopher Hannah Arendt used the phrase "the banality of evil" in discussing Eichmann and his career in her book *Eichmann in Jerusalem*, a report and reflection on his trial in Israel in 1961.

Arendt was illustrating, through Eichmann, her thesis of an earlier book, *The Origins of Totalitarianism*, that depersonalization was an important aspect of the growth of totalitarianism (of which Nazism was one variety) in the modern world. However, her theory was not applicable to Eichmann. At his trial Eichmann tried to present himself as an underling, forced to carry out orders, a defense used by many other war criminals. The fact is that although Eichmann never rose above the rank of *Obersturmbannführer* (lieutenant colonel) and had no input into the grand design of the Final Solution, he was a Nazi "idealist," passionately committed to the genocide program, and a perfectionist about erasing every last Jew, making sure to include children.

"Eichmann's mind was set on the liquidation of Hungarian Jews long before Hitler even thought about the occupation of Hungary," states Randolph L. Braham in his monograph, *Eichmann and the Destruction of Hungarian Jewry*. Braham points out that in 1942 the Hungarian general József Heszlényi proposed a plan to deport one hundred thousand "alien" Jews from Hungary to Transnistria, a barren waste in the Ukraine, but that when the plan was submitted to

Eichmann, who was in charge of transportation, he decided that it was not worthwhile to put the entire machinery of deportation into gear for so small a number. In a letter to the legal expert of his department, Kurt Klingenfus, he said it would be best to wait until all the Jews of Hungary could be taken care of.

In the interview with Dutch journalist Wilhelm Sassen in Argentina in 1953, Eichmann described himself as afire with Nazi ideology, and reported that his chief, Reinhard Heydrich, had encouraged him to study Jews, their customs and organization. He managed to wangle an assignment in Palestine in 1937 and met with Arab leaders there. He tried to study Hebrew and Yiddish on his own when he was denied funds to hire a teacher. Although he never gained as great a facility in the languages as he boasted, he learned enough to impress his superiors and cause anxiety to captive Jews who wanted to communicate something to one another in his presence.

Eichmann felt particular enthusiasm for his project in Hungary. He had nearly ten years of experience in dealing with Jewish "emigration" and related issues, and for a year and a half had been in charge of transportation of Jews from all over Europe to the death camps, but he had never before worked in the field. More than a half dozen of his closest collaborators over the years were brought to Budapest to work with him on the dejewification of Hungary. He felt challenged to do a clean, swift job. He wanted no Warsaw ghetto type of uprising in Hungary.

But there was never any real danger of such an uprising in Hungary. In the first place, there was a lack of young, strong men to fight. Most of the men between eighteen and thirty-five were serving in forced-labor service companies throughout the country and along the frontier. The leaders of the Jewish community in Budapest were by age, temperament and outlook incapable of armed resistance. Most of them were businessmen and lawyers, accustomed to appeals, compromise and solutions to problems. In the country as a whole, Jews were divided. They came from widely divergent perspectives ranging from the extremely Orthodox (Hasidic in some areas) to the most secular and assimilated. In the Neolog (Reform) community there was a strain of superpatriotism. There had been Jewish communities in Hungary for more than a thousand years. Jews were among the most ardent followers of Hungary's national liberationist, Louis Kossuth. They had a distinguished record of service in World War I, and many held medals for heroism. They had won civil and political advances by defining themselves as Magyars first and Jews second.

Among the assimilated group, many had family ties in Hungarian aristocracy and were married to gentiles. More than 150,000 who had converted to Christianity were defined as Jews according to racial laws passed in 1938, 1939 and 1941. Those born of Jewish parents after 1919, or having two Jewish grandparents, were considered Jewish despite their conversions.

The Hungarian Jews were, by and large, conservative and little deserved the Bolshevik label pinned on them by violent anti-Semites in the country. After World War I Hungary lost two thirds of her territory as a result of the Trianon Peace Treaty. During the postwar political and economic upheaval, a Bolshevik regime headed by Béla Kun—a Hungarian of Jewish background, trained in Russia—took over. He placed his followers, many of them of Jewish origin, in high positions and proceeded to try to transform the country overnight. His Red Terror regime lasted six months and was then overturned by the White Terror, which brought in violent, rightist, anti-Semitic uprisings.

A counterrevolutionary government headed by Hungary's great war hero, Admiral Miklós Horthy, took over. As regent, Horthy had great power. He appointed and dismissed the prime minister. He could convene, adjourn and dissolve parliament and could exercise a suspensive veto of laws passed by the parliament. Despite his avowed anti-Semitism, he recognized the need for the Jews in a country made up of a landed aristocracy, peasants, and civil servants who were the younger, unpropertied sons of the aristocrats. The Jews made up the indispensable middle class. Although they represented only about 5 percent of the population, they constituted about half the country's independent businessmen, doctors and lawyers. They were represented in engineering, science and writing by more than 30 percent. They were predominant in banking and accounting. In Budapest, where the Jews represented about 30 percent of the population, a high percentage were in journalism and the arts. And in the fighting forces Jews were desperately needed as doctors, veterinarians, engineers and vehicle drivers. However, not all Jews were well off. There were also many poor Jews in the countryside.

Despite the violent anti-Semitism that followed the Kun regime and despite the quota imposed on Jewish admission to institutions of higher learning in 1920, Hungarian Jews hoped that economic aid to their country would bring about a change of climate. When American Jews showed concern about the violation of Hungary's treaty agreement to respect civil rights, the Hungarian Jews urged them to use their influence instead to redress the wrongs of Trianon.

Help finally came to Hungary from the wrong quarter. When Hitler came to power in 1933 he immediately started courting Hungary with loans and technical assistance. He also inundated the country with student propagandists, agents and journalists. The result was a proliferation of anti-Semitic propaganda organs and an active spy network which planted supporters in the police, the gendarmerie and the regent's office.

With the onset of the war, Hungary became an Axis supporter and in return received a gift from Hitler of substantial slices of her lost territories. Nevertheless, some moderate forces remained in the government, and there was some anti-German resistance. For five years Hungarian Jews experienced shock waves of hope and despair as the country went through six different premiers, some ardently pro-German and others uneasy about total German domination. On one hand, thousands of Jewish refugees were allowed to remain in the country, and the government resisted repeated German demands to find "a solution to the Jewish problem"—for example, deport the Jews. On the other, severe economic and professional restrictions were imposed on Jews, depriving them of their livelihoods. In addition, Jewish men were excluded from the armed forces, but had to serve in labor service companies in which they did construction work and handled freight for the Army. They were severely abused. When Hungary joined the war against Russia, they were sent into the Ukraine without proper clothing in the winter of 1942–43, where they died by the thousands of cold, starvation and disease.

In January 1943, the Second Hungarian Army serving on the eastern front at the Don River received a devastating defeat at the hands of the Russians and made a frantic retreat. It was noted by Hungarian General Gustav Jany that, in contrast to the army, the Jewish labor companies preserved order and picked up the dead and wounded. About six thousand or seven thousand labor service men out of forty thousand survived the battle.

Hitler was badly disillusioned with the Hungarians, and Horthy was disenchanted with Hitler. He wanted to get the country out of the war and keep the advancing Russians out of Hungary. He made peace feelers to the Western Allies. Hitler knew about his efforts and he sent his Central European expert, Edmund Veesenmayer, on two separate missions to find out what was wrong with Hungary. Veesenmayer spotted the major problem: Jews. They were everywhere—in business, in the cultural and professional life. In his second report he noted that there were 1.1 million Jews in the country, and they were "saboteurs" and "Bolshevik vanguards." He recommended immediate action on the Jewish question.

On March 17, 1944, Hitler invited Horthy to his mountain retreat at Schloss Klessheim. He raged against him and told Horthy he must get rid of his liberal Prime Minister Miklós Kállay, who had been actively promoting a peace agreement with the West, believing that the British and American forces were eager to come into the Balkans. Furthermore, Hitler demanded that Horthy deal at once with the "Jewish problem." Horthy, seventy years old and accustomed to the deference paid to near royalty, dashed out of the room in a fury. On the way home to Hungary, he discovered that a special car had been attached to his private train. It contained Veesenmayer, who was appointed to serve in Hungary as Reich plenipotentiary, and a formidable staff of political and propaganda experts. In Horthy's two-day absence his country was occupied by eleven German divisions. A parachute regiment had first been dropped into the country near Budapest. There was virtually no resistance from the Hungarians.

Along with the occupation troops came SS and Gestapo units. Eichmann's *Sonderkommando* (special commando) consisted of no more than two hundred men. Eichmann planned to have the Hungarians execute the deportation program and found the perfect administrators in László Endre and László Baky, two notorious anti-Semites who were appointed secretaries of state under the newly formed German-approved government. Horthy appointed Döme Sztójay as prime minister, with Veesenmayer's approval.

The Germans arrived on Sunday, March 19, with a list of names of prominent Jews and anti-Nazis. They arrested 3,451 leaders in the areas of politics, business, law and the press. They threw them into hastily set-up internment camps. They also rounded up thousands of Jews who were found at railroad and boat terminals, and for good measure took names of Jewish doctors and lawyers out of the telephone book, rounded them up and threw these people into camps. There was a wave of suicides in Budapest.

This psychological blitzkrieg was followed by an order to form a Jewish Council, which would represent all elements of the community—the Orthodox, Neolog (liberal or Reform) and Zionist. They were to publish a newspaper subject to Gestapo censorship. They were to urge the Jewish masses to be calm and to assure them that no harm would come to them if they obeyed orders. They also received a strange set of demands. The Germans wanted cocktail shakers, glassware, silverware, kitchen equipment including mops and pails, typewriters, women's lingerie, perfume, Watteau paintings and a piano. All the demands were promptly fulfilled. However, the following day the Germans demanded three hundred mattresses, six hundred blankets and thirty compositors. The Jews protested they didn't know where to acquire so many supplies on immediate demand. A German officer retorted that if it was possible to execute ten thousand Jews in ten minutes, it should be a simple matter to supply the equipment. The demands were quickly fulfilled.

Eichmann did not meet with the selected members of the Jewish Council until March 31. He strutted before them in jackboots and warned against any effort to deceive him. He boasted of his knowledge of Hebrew and Yiddish and Jewish customs and communal life, and asked for a tour of the Jewish archives in Budapest. He wanted the finances of all Hungarian Jews placed under jurisdiction of the Central Council (this included converts to Christianity, whom he claimed were the richest). The Jews were not to try to link with any partisans, and Eichmann in turn would see that no abuses would be perpetrated against them. He ordered that every Jew of Hungary was to start wearing a yellow star on April 5. The exact size and color were specified. It was to be worn on the left breast, clearly visible at all times.

Despite the dire warnings of the refugees from Poland and Slovakia, and despite their own apprehensions, the leaders of the Jewish community did not fully comprehend the significance of the yellow star. It was used not merely to humiliate the Jews and isolate them from the general population: It was a death mark.

In retrospect it would seem that if the Jews had simply refused to put on the yellow star, the Germans would have been confronted with so much hopeless confusion they could not possibly have carried out their extermination program. There undoubtedly would have been massacres, but they could not have killed hundreds of thousands. However, neither the masses nor their leaders saw any alternative at the time but to obey the Germans. The Jewish Council appealed to the Hungarian government, but was told that it must deal with the Germans. Horthy had promised Hitler to turn over Jews for "labor," and the Germans insisted that the Jews were going to labor camps. When they were asked why, in that case, whole families had to be deported, the Nazis responded that it was in deference to the close family ties among Jews.

Jewish Council head Samu Stern stated after the war that if the council had refused to obey the German commands to urge people to remain calm, they would simply have been deported and killed, and others would have been found to take their place. He considered it his duty to remain at his post. He believed that the war would soon end with the defeat of the Nazis. He said he was not fooled by the Germans, but felt it was a matter of "a race with time." At that moment it seemed important to keep up people's hopes and spirits. Kossuth Radio, the resistance station beamed from Moscow, urged the Jews, "Wear your yellow stars proudly." Author Elie Wiesel, whose father was the leader of the Orthodox community of Sighet in Northern Transylvania, recalls in his memoir *Night* that his father said, "The yellow star? Oh well, what of it? You won't die of it." Of course, he was wrong.

Despite their profound knowledge of anti-Semitism and the already advanced stage of the Holocaust, it was beyond the imagination of pious, unworldly people who devoted their lives to Torah study that a cold-blooded plan existed to extinguish not only the Hungarian Jews but all the Jews in Europe.

Eichmann's plan was simple. With the help of his Hungarian henchmen he divided Hungary into six zones. The Jews in each zone were to be driven from their homes and ghettoized systematically. Those in tiny communities—some having as few as two or three Jews— were to be taken to larger centers. They were to be stripped of property and held to await deportation. The first zones to be emptied were the Carpatho-Ruthenia region in northeastern Hungary and Northern Transylvania, and the last was to be Budapest.

Baky and Endre worked with Eichmann's officers in supervising the gendarmerie, who were under the command of Lieutenant-Colonel László Ferenczy. They all approached their task with enthusiasm and efficiency.

The step-by-step stripping of Jewish dignity, property and finally life itself was poignantly described in her diary by a 16-year-old girl named Éva Heyman, who lived with her grandparents in Nagyvarad, a city with the largest Jewish population in Transylvania, more than 21,000. Éva's parents were divorced. Her father had converted to Catholicism and her mother had remarried a noted former deputy of the Hungarian Parliament and fiction writer, Béla Zsolt. Her parents had both come from families of Neolog rabbis, but her mother and her second husband were socialists with a universalist outlook. Eva noted in her diary which she started at age thirteen that her ambition was to be a news photographer and to marry an "Aryan Englishman."*

Éva's diary was preserved by Mariska, the Christian maid of the family, to whom she was deeply attached. The entry for April 7 reads:

Today they came for my bicycle. I almost caused a big drama. You know, dear diary, I was awfully afraid just by the fact that the policemen came into the house. I know that policemen bring only trouble with them, wherever they go. My bicycle had a proper license plate, and Grandpa had paid the tax for it. That's how the policemen found it, because it was registered at City Hall that I have a bicycle. Now that it's all over, I'm so ashamed about how I behaved in front of the policemen. So, dear diary, I threw myself on the ground, held on to the back wheel of my bicycle, and shouted all sorts of things at the policemen: "Shame on you for taking away a bicycle from a girl. That's robbery." We had saved up for a year and a half to buy the bicycle. We had sold my old bicycle, my layette and Grandpa's old winter coat and added the money we saved. My grandparents, Juszti [her governess], the Agis [her mother and her aunt], Grandma Lujza and Papa all had chipped in to buy my bicycle. We still didn't have the whole sum, but Hoffmann didn't sell the bicycle to anyone else, and he even said that I could take the bicycle home. My father would pay, or Grandpa. But I didn't want to take the bicycle home until we had all the money. But in the meantime I hurried over to the store whenever I could and looked to see if that red bicycle was still there. How Agi [her mother] laughed when I told her that when the whole sum was finally there. I went to the store and took the bicycle home, only I didn't ride it but led it along with my hands, the way you handle a big, beautiful dog. From the outside I admired the bicycle, and

---

*The diary was published by Yad Vashem, Jerusalem, in a translation by Moshe Kohn, with notes by Judah Marton, in 1974.

even gave it a name: Friday. I took the name from Robinson Crusoe, but it suits the bicycle....

One of the policemen was very annoyed and said: All we need is for a Jewgirl to put on such a comedy when her bicycle is being taken away. No Jewkid is entitled to keep a bicycle anymore. The Jews aren't entitled to bread, either; they shouldn't guzzle everything, but leave the food for the soldiers. You can imagine, dear diary, how I felt when they were saying this to my face. I had only heard that sort of thing on the radio, or read it in a German newspaper. Still, it's different when you read something and when it's thrown into your face....

But you know, dear diary, I think the other policeman felt sorry for me. You should be ashamed of yourself, colleague, he said, is your heart made of stone? How can you speak that way to such a beautiful girl? Then he stroked my hair and promised to take good care of my bicycle. He gave me a receipt and told me not to cry, because when the war was over I would get my bicycle back. At worst it would need some repairs at Hoffmann's.

While the Easter bells rang over the countryside, at a time when the Jews would normally be preparing for their Passover holiday, the gendarmes were searching Jewish homes for valuables and driving the occupants out. Homes left empty and unlocked were further looted by neighbors.

Éva was subsequently to be exposed to the stripping of her grandparents' home: "Now the apartment isn't pretty any more. All the beautiful things in it they have taken away. The silverware, the rugs, the paintings, the Venetian mirror. They left a receipt for the rugs, but even Grandpa says we will never get them back." Eventually, even the gold chain that held the key to Éva's diary was taken, but Éva found a bit of velvet ribbon to replace it. She entered the ghetto carrying her diary and her canary in a cage.

The ghettos were usually set up in synagogues or huge open spaces without protection or sanitary facilities. Very little food or water was distributed. People tried to carry as much as they could with them. Men, women and young girls were subjected to brutal body searches for jewelry. Children had to watch their parents and grandparents beaten and tortured. There were many suicides and attempts at suicide. Éva learned that the screams in the night came from people who were being tortured to reveal where their possessions had been hidden.

In her final diary entry, on May 30, Éva writes:

It's no use that everybody says that we're not going to Poland, but to Balaton.... Dear diary, I don't want to die; I want to live even if it means that I'll be the only person here allowed to stay. I would wait for the end in some cellar, or on the roof, or in some secret cranny. I would even let the cross-eyed gendarme, the one who took our flour away from us, kiss me, just as long as they didn't kill me, only that they should let me live.

Before Éva and her grandparents were driven into the cattle cars, she ran to the maid, Mariska, to give her the diary and the canary. Éva's mother and stepfather had been smuggled out of the ghetto during the night and had fled to Budapest. Few gentiles had the will and/or courage to come to the aid of the Jews. The man or woman who brought food or water to the ghetto risked a beating from the gendarmes.

Town by town, area by area, was systematically emptied of Jews. There were few instances of resistance. Resistors were promptly shot. Jews were pulled out of jails, mental institutions and hospitals and thrown into the cattle cars with the others. Included were people who had just had operations and newborn babies with their mothers. They were dumped, eighty to a car and given two buckets, one filled with water, the other for waste. The cars were sealed and the trains rode over the hot countryside toward Auschwitz, a journey of from two or three days to a week, depending on the departure point.

Some wealthy and influential Jews were able to bribe their way into hiding, but many paid the bribe price and then were betrayed. The Germans seized valuable paintings, antiques, tapestries and jewelry and shipped them to Germany—much to the chagrin of the Hungarians, who were left with only some of the loot from middle-class homes. In addition, the Germans wanted to be paid for their job of dejewifying Hungary. They demanded and received the food rations of the deported Jews, plus two billion pengos (about four million dollars) to cover the transportation costs of the deportations.

The most sensational acquisition by the Germans was the huge Weiss-Manfred Works of Cespel, which specialized in heavy materials and armaments, but also had banking, mining and other industrial interests. Both Hermann Göring, chief of the Luftwaffe, and Heinrich Himmler, chief of the SS, had eyes on the company. The business was owned by four families of Jewish origin (many of them converted to

Christianity) linked by marriage to Christians, among them members of the aristocracy. In the wake of anti-Jewish legislation in the thirties, the company's holdings had been consolidated into a trust company; 51 percent of the shares were held in the names of Aryan members of the family.

Himmler's clever economic representative, Kurt Becher, quickly started negotiations with the families early in April and by mid-May succeeded in acquiring the controlling majority of shares in the entire industry for the SS. The Jewish-owned shares would automatically go to the Hungarian government. Forty-seven members of the family were taken by train and plane out of the country in May and June and eventually reached Lisbon, where they were discovered by the press, which reported the arrival of Hungarian millionaires carrying great quantities of gold. Nine members of the family were held as hostages in Vienna to insure the "good behavior" of those who were freed.

While the Weiss-Chorins, the families who owned the Weiss-Manfred enterprise, had unique power to escape the murder machinery, rescue operations for ordinary Jews were pitifully scarce and hazardous. The only effective project was run by Zionists, who in 1943 organized the *Vaadat Ezra ve'Hazalah,* the Relief and Rescue Committee. Known as the Vaada, they ran a daring rescue operation, supplying false "Aryan" papers and smuggling Jews across the borders—first into Hungary from Poland, Slovakia, Austria and Germany, and later out of Hungary via Romania and Turkey for "illegal" transportation to Palestine. They often encountered resistance when they urged people to flee for their lives. People preferred to believe the Nazi lie that they were being transported to labor camps. The Vaada had all the information about what was going on in the death camps, and they ran an active courier service getting information to and from Istanbul.

An Orthodox rabbi in Slovakia, Michael Beer-Dov Weissmandel, teamed with a Zionist woman leader, Gisi Fleischmann, in a project that aimed to rescue children and to inform the world about the mass murders. In 1943 they had given Dieter Wisliceny, Eichmann's aide in charge of deportations in Slovakia, a bribe of fifty thousand dollars to stop the deportations from the country. The deportations stopped. Believing their bribe had been effective, they worked up a proposal known as the Europa Plan to save all the remaining Jews of Europe.

Wisliceny went to Berlin and came back with a price—two million dollars. (After the war, Wisliceny testified that he had discussed the project with Eichmann, who named the figure.)

However, the Jews of the free world did not trust the Nazis, and despite the exhortations of the rabbi, little money was raised.

Weissmandel and Fleischmann were probably wrong about the effectiveness of their bribe. It is now believed that a demand from the Catholic bishops of Slovakia to see the camps, to which two thirds of the Slovakian Jewish community had already been deported, caused the Germans to back off—for the moment. They later returned for the surviving Slovakian Jews. However, Weissmandel gave Wisliceny a letter in Hebrew to the Orthodox leaders of Budapest indicating that Wisliceny was a man who could be dealt with.

Wisliceny was contacted by two Zionist leaders, Rudolf Kasztner and Joel Brand, who had succeeded in rescuing individuals from camps and deportations through bribery. At a meeting on March 25 he offered the opportunity to save "the substance" of Hungarian Jewry for two million dollars. What did "the substance" mean? Wisliceny was cryptic— "the biological base." Several more meetings took place involving other members of the Eichmann command. While the Jews were being herded into ghettos, a deposit of three million Hungarian pengos, and a second installment of two and a half million pengos, were turned over to the Nazis. The deposit money had been collected by Samu Stern, head of the Jewish Council.

Despite these negotiations, on April 24 Eichmann and Endre toured the ghettos in the northeastern part of the country and found everything satisfactory: The deportations could begin.

The following day Eichmann ordered Joel Brand to be picked up and brought to him, and the curtain went up on the first scene of one of the most complex and painful dramas of the Holocaust in Hungary. Thousands of articles and many books have been written about the "blood for trucks" proposal that Eichmann made to Joel Brand that day, but there are still unexplained facets of the story. The repercussions of Eichmann's offer and conflicting accounts of the actions of Kasztner, Brand and others in the Vaada caused guilt, recriminations, accusations, soul-searching for decades. In 1953 the case surfaced in a sensational eight-month trial in Israel which led to the fall of a government and finally to Kasztner's assassination.

Eichmann said he could spare one million Jews for a price. The price was "goods"—coffee, tea, chemicals, soap, trucks. Eichmann was somewhat offhand about numbers. He tentatively suggested about one hundred Jews for a truck. The trucks were to be winterized, indicating they were to be used on the eastern front. Eichmann asked what kind of Jews Brand wanted—young men and women ("the biological base"), or children and older people. Brand said he wanted all of them. Eichmann said he could arrange for Brand to go abroad to bring the offer to international Jewry who, according to the Nazi version of reality, controlled the Allies.

Two or three subsequent meetings were held and finally visa arrangements were made for Brand to go to Istanbul. The Jewish Agency in Istanbul had been contacted about the mission and had responded that "Chaim" was awaiting the emissary. Brand was ordered to return as quickly as he could with a concrete reply. Brand estimated that this might take a week or two. He was given to understand by Eichmann that if he failed to return with an answer in a reasonable length of time, he would be forfeiting the lives of his wife and children, along with all the Jews of Hungary.

Brand left on May 17, two days after the deportations from Northern Transylvania began. Eichmann sent Brand with a "shadow"—a man named Andor "Bandi" Grosz. Grosz was a convert from Judaism, a convicted smuggler who had served the German and Hungarian espionage units and had also acted as a courier for the Vaada.

The Jewish leaders heard the news with dismay. They did not consider Brand the best-qualified person for so important a mission. Furthermore, the presence of a disreputable character like Grosz threw a dubious cast over the project.

Scholars have speculated about Eichmann's purpose in sending Grosz, and one of the more likely possibilities is that he wanted to sabotage the mission. Eichmann took his orders directly from Himmler, but he balked whenever he saw a possibility of Jews escaping the net.

Himmler had noted the creation of the American War Refugee Board and recognized that the United States was becoming seriously interested in rescuing Jews. He could see that the war was turning against Germany and knew that forces in Germany were conspiring against Hitler. Himmler could now take advantage of the considerable power he had personally acquired and, using the Jews as a wedge, open negotiations to make an armistice with the West. Eichmann, on the other hand, did not have so long a vision or so demonically creative a mind as Himmler. He was single-mindedly focused on destroying Jews.

Trouble plagued Brand from the moment he left. There were visa difficulties in Istanbul. Then the "Chaim" who awaited him was not the one he expected—Chaim Weizmann, head of the World Zionist Organization—but a lesser personage, Chaim Barlas of the Jewish Agency's Istanbul office. After many mishaps and after being taken prisoner by British Intelligence, which saw only Nazi intrigue in Brand's story, the hapless emissary finally met with Moshe Shertok, head of the Jewish Agency in Palestine, and Ira Hirschmann, President Roosevelt's personal emissary. The interview with the latter was conducted in Cairo, where by mid-June Joel Brand was being held under house arrest by the British. Both Shertok and Hirschmann judged the offer bona fide and suggested that negotiations be opened with a view to stopping immediately the deportations in Hungary, as well as the gassings, which were continuing on a round-the-clock basis in Auschwitz.

Instead of opening negotiations, the British and American governments decided to tell the Russians about the offer and ask for their assent. They received their answer on June 20. Deputy Soviet Foreign Minister Andrei Vishinsky thought it was neither expedient nor permissible to negotiate with the Germans on such a matter. And that was that.

When Brand did not return and sent only a cryptic message that he was working on the arrangements, Kasztner and Brand's wife, Hansi, took up the negotiations with Eichmann. They tried to persuade him to halt the deportations, insisting it was only a matter of time—a response from the Jews in the free world would be forthcoming. They failed to get him to hold the deportations, but he agreed that six hundred holders of immigration certificates to Palestine could leave for any neutral or Allied-controlled country. They could not be sent to Palestine, Eichmann declared, because the Arabs would protest. In fact, the Grand Mufti, living in Berlin at that time, sent Horthy a strong protest against the planned emigration of orphan children.

As a result of a separate agreement with Eichmann, 388 "prominent" Jews who were being interned preparatory to deportation in the ghetto of Kolozsvár were brought to a camp in Budapest pending their departure. Among the noted rabbis and scholars and Zionist leaders in the group were Kasztner's own family and friends.

Kasztner and Mrs. Brand continued their negotiations with Eichmann, asking for another hundred thousand Jews in return for jewelry, foreign currency and pengos worth five million Swiss francs.

The best they could get was an agreement to send thirty thousand Jews to family work camps in Austria. About twenty thousand were actually sent and three quarters of this group survived the war.

The ghettoization and deportations continued throughout May and June, and word got back to Budapest about the horrors being perpetrated on the Jews of the countryside. They were the parents and grandparents, the sisters and brothers, aunts and uncles and cousins of the Budapest Jews, who realized—too late—that they had been misled into obedience. But they still saw no way out. A petition sent to Hungarian professors and intellectuals only brought the arrest of the perpetrators. The noted filmmaker Béla Pásztor made an emotional speech at a mass meeting in the Dohanyi Street Synagogue late in June, calling upon the community to rise and take up arms. He was met by silence. Where were the arms and who was to take them up?

Finally, toward the end of June, an appeal to the Hungarian government to allow 300 to 400 holders of Swedish emigration passports and 7,000 holders of Palestine certificates to leave the country brought a favorable response. However, the Council of Ministers declared it would seek the response of the Reich government on the matter.

In the meantime, Horthy became aware that his Under Secretary of State László Baky was planning a coup. This fact, added to the protests from neutrals, Allies and the Papal Nuncio, plus the Allies' successful landing in Normandy and their increased air power over Hungary, led him to cancel the deportations and decide to bring in a new, less pro-German prime minister, Géza Lakatos.

On the night of June 30 the special train for which Kasztner had arranged left Budapest during an air raid. There were supposed to be 1,300 on board, but in the confusion of the raid, stowaways climbed aboard and the train left with 1,684 persons. The train arrived at Bergen-Belsen on July 8, and the passengers were held under special conditions not far from the notorious camp, where some of their less lucky coreligionists were being held. Bergen-Belsen was not a death camp, although thousands died there of starvation and disease.

The tragedy of the helplessness of the Hungarian Jews is perhaps best epitomized in the story of three young Zionists who flew from Palestine to try to save them. One of them was Hannah Szenes, the twenty-three-year-old daughter of a noted Hungarian playwright. She had grown up in an assimilated household and attended a Protestant school, but turned to Zionism under the impact of a growing anti-Semitism around her. After her graduation from high school, she left for a kibbutz in Palestine, and could have remained there safely doing agricultural work for the remainder of the war.

However, she feared for her mother and younger brother in Hungary. She urged them to join her. Her brother managed to get a visa, but her mother did not. Hannah became one of a group of thirty-two who volunteered for a special mission for the British army. The group consisted of young people from the Balkans who would be parachuted into enemy country to work with the partisans and send messages to Allied airmen. They were committed to executing the military part of their mission before they attempted any rescue work.

Hannah and her comrades parachuted into Yugoslavia in March, and then they separated into groups. They lived among the partisans in the woods of Yugoslavia. Hannah learned there that Hungary had been occupied by the Germans and quickly crossed the border with her partner, Joel Nussbecher. She was caught by a Hungarian border guard on June 9. Her transmitter was found and she was brought into prison in Budapest. She was beaten to reveal her radio code and the names of the people she was supposed to contact in Budapest, but she kept her silence. And so did Joel, who was also captured.

On July 9, when the roundup for the Budapest deportation was supposed to begin, she was one of approximately 230,000 Jews in the city who knew they were among the last Jews left in the country. Some 150,000 men were scattered in labor-service companies.

Eichmann's job had been substantially completed before Wallenberg arrived in Budapest.

SEVEN

HOPE FOR THE DOOMED

Budapest was very different from the city Wallenberg had seen a year earlier. A heavy air raid on July 2 struck outlying industrial centers, but had also left some buildings shattered and windows broken in the heart of the capital. Despite the summer sunlight there was a pall over the city.

Nearly one fourth of Budapest's inhabitants were locked up in their star-marked houses through most of the day. Jewish businesses throughout the city were boarded up and marked with the six-pointed star. When the Jews appeared in the streets in the permitted time between 2 and 5 P.M., their pale, haunted faces and the bright yellow star on their breasts made them appear like creatures from another world—both frightened and frightening.

The radio and newspapers were bombarding the Hungarian people with the idea that these apparitions, once their fellow citizens, were responsible for the air raids from the West and the advancing "Bolshevik menace," also known as the "Judeo-Bolshevik menace," from the East. They were also blamed for the food shortages and the black market.

In the brief time they were allowed out of their houses, the Jews had to hurry about trying to get food and medical attention, visiting the ill and elderly, trying to visit the neutral embassies to get some sort of special passport that might provide protection against deportation and, most important, trying to get news.

What was happening? Was the July 10 deportation from Budapest really off? What did that mean? Would another one soon be scheduled? Where were the people from the suburbs of Budapest taken? What had happened to the train with fifteen hundred important and lucky people on it? Had they really been taken to Switzerland? And would thousands of families really be shipped out to Palestine? Who had disappeared in the last few days? Were they arrested or in hiding? Had anyone received word from a deportee? Yes? Postcards from a place called Waldsee? They were well and working? But where was Waldsee? It was rumored someone had received a card signed *R'evim* (Hebrew for hungry) and another signed *Blimalbish* (Hebrew for without clothing). What were they really doing with those people? It couldn't be true, what some said, about gassings. No! That would be insane! They dimly grasped the truth: Jews slated for death had been forced to write the cards. Waldsee was a fiction.

Wallenberg arrived, weary from his all-night voyage sitting on his two knapsacks in the train filled with chattering, bantering young German soldiers returning from furlough. They boasted about their sexual conquests at home, fighting their fears about what lay ahead. Those going to the eastern front knew by now that they faced a tough foe, one with good reason to feel nothing but implacable hatred for Germans.

Wallenberg went directly from the station to the Swedish legation on Gyopér Street, high on Gellért Hill in Buda. He noted the long line of people wearing yellow stars, waiting patiently in front of the building. The word had gotten out that the Swedish legation was giving certain documents to Jews who were supposedly planning to emigrate and become Swedish citizens or to travel in Sweden. It was virtually impossible to do either under the prevailing war conditions, but the Swedes and the Jews hoped the papers would provide some protection against deportation.

Wallenberg was warmly greeted by Per Anger, a legation attaché who was also an old friend and who welcomed help at the overburdened diplomatic headquarters. Contrasted with tall, blond, blue-eyed, well-tailored Per Anger, Wallenberg's appearance was undistinguished. His medium height, prematurely balding head and his usually unassuming manner suggested an academic man rather than a diplomat. But there were contradicitons about him. He had the poise and polish of a worldly Swedish aristocrat, but the intensity of his eyes and the sensitive modeling of his mouth suggested a character that did not fit into social molds. He looked at once vulnerable and highly controlled. Inside him was a demon of still-unleashed creative energies. Neither he nor anyone else knew his full capabilities at that time. There was still a boyish diffidence about him. He showed Anger his revolver, half amused at himself. "It's just to give me courage," he explained. "I'll never use it. I'm really a coward."

Anger briefed Wallenberg on what the Swedes had been doing. The small staff represented a legation rather than an embassy. It had been increased by the addition of Valdemar Langlet and his wife, Nina, as representatives of the Swedish Red Cross. Langlet, a professor of Swedish in Budapest, had managed to find hiding places in convents and other church institutions for a small number of children, and provided a "letter of protection" under the Swedish Red Cross for several hundred individuals. In addition, the legation had issued about seven hundred provisional passports to individuals with Swedish connections or travel plans.

Nobody was sure at first how helpful these documents might be, but just before Wallenberg arrived, two Budapest businessmen put the matter to a test. One of them, Hugo Wohl, had gone so far as to hire a lawyer to argue his case before the Hungarian authorities. He claimed that his Swedish provisional passport made him a Swedish citizen, and therefore he was not subject to the order that all Hungarian Jews must live in yellow-star houses and wear the yellow star. He won the case and was exempted! Wilhelm Forgács, who had been working in a forced-labor company, had been rounded up, along with other Jews, for deportation. He presented his Swedish document to an officer, who was uncertain but afraid to do the wrong thing. He put Forgács in an internment camp; later the Swedes were able to get him out.

Wallenberg considered these two stories carefully. They offered amazing insight into the psychology of bureaucracy. People ready to send their fellow humans off to untold suffering and death without a qualm could be stopped dead by the sight of an official-looking document. This was something to build on! He recognized that a small dent had appeared in the machinery of destruction. He would widen it as much as possible.

Wallenberg proceeded to use his art training to design a document of particularly impressive appearance. It bore the Swedish three-crowns emblem, colored in blue and yellow, and carried a picture of the bearer. It stated that the bearer was, in effect, provisionally a Swede. He or she was going to emigrate to Sweden and was, therefore, under Swedish protection. It was signed by Ambassador Danielsson and by Wallenberg. The document was called a *Schutzpass*, or protective passport. There was nothing understated about its "official" look. Wallenberg aimed at a strong psychological impact.

The new legation attaché then set out to hire a staff for his section C, charged with protection of Jewish interests. He at once hired Forgács and Wohl. They had the kind of courage and initiative he needed. He quickly built up a staff of forty whose first job it would be to distribute as many *Schutzpässe* as possible. He managed to secure immunity from wearing the yellow star for his staff members. This enabled them to move about freely at all hours of the day. It also exempted them from labor service.

During his first week in Budapest, Wallenberg also went to visit Horthy, the great Hungarian military and political hero, bearing a letter from King Gustav. The tall seventy-six-year-old regent, sitting in the Hapsburg splendor of his palace, must have been a bit astounded at the thirty-two-year-old Swede delivering his lecture on humanitarianism. Wallenberg wrote home to his mother that despite Horthy's great height, "I felt taller than he was." The importance of the interview lay in the fact that Wallenberg made Horthy aware that Sweden was committed to trying to prevent any further atrocities to Jews. If he permitted them, he would have some serious accounting to do after the war.

Wallenberg then went on to introduce himself to the Jewish community, bearing his letter to Samu Stern from Rabbi Ehrenpreis. When Wallenberg turned up at Jewish Council headquarters at 12 Sip Street, the Jewish leaders had mixed feelings. They had felt isolated and deserted during the months in which disaster had struck the community. Then a young Swede entered as the curtain was about to fall on the last act of the tragedy, saying he had come to help them. What could one nice young man do against the German juggernaut? However, when they discovered Wallenberg's total dedication and his enormous capacity for work, they were won over.

In an account written at the end of the war, Stern described Wallenberg as "unselfish, full of endless élan and the will to work like all great men." He added that Wallenberg's example induced others—the Swiss, the Portuguese, the Spanish and the Vatican—to emulate his activities.

Wallenberg saw the despair of the Jews and said in one of his early reports to Stockholm (July 29), "It is necessary to rouse the Jews from their apathy." He wanted also

to relieve them of the feeling that they had been abandoned. In this respect the intervention of King Gustav has been of real help. Interventions of the same sort from other foreign institutions would carry enormous weight and would make those to whom they are addressed, reflect. I suggest that the archbishop of Sweden send a message to the Hungarian bishops.

He noted that the radio reports from the Western allies kept threatening those responsible for war crimes, but he felt they should also offer clemency to those who change their attitude, and should promise to help those who protect Jews.

By a happy coincidence, the first person Wallenberg met at council headquarters was László Petö, the son of Ernö Petö, deputy president of the Jewish community of Pest. Wallenberg and László had met years earlier when they were students at a hostel in Thenon-les-Bains, France. Wallenberg became a frequent guest in the Petö home.

The Petö home provided a good source of news. Wallenberg must have quickly learned that Petö was in regular contact with Horthy, Jr. Petö's son-in-law had once been Horthy, Jr.'s, secretary at a diplomatic post in Brazil. Petö used this association to establish contact with the young man. In an account written at the end of the war, Petö said he met with Horthy, Jr., at frequent intervals from mid-June through mid-October. Horthy, Jr., defended his father by saying he had been lied to about the deportations by his ministers. Horthy, Jr., also met with Ottó Komoly, the president of the Hungarian Zionist Association. In Komoly's postwar account, young Horthy told him:

By birth and upbringing I am an anti-Semite. It could not have been different with us in view of the way they spoke about Jews in our parents' home. For example, it would be inconceivable for me to marry a Jewish woman or for my children to have Jewish blood.

But then I got involved in economic life. I saw what happened there.... Our civil servants have no feeling for the economic interests of the country. As far as they are concerned, the country could go bankrupt.

This is why there is a need for the Jews, who, while looking after their own interests, have advanced the interests of the country.... As a sportsman, I know that peak results can only bē obtained through competition. The Hungarians need the competition the Jews represent. The extent of Jewish emigration must be regulated in accordance with the interests of the nation.

Through Petö and other sources Wallenberg learned about the desperate efforts the Budapest Jews were making to deal with the German and Hungarian authorities in order to stall further deportations. They were functioning from the edge of a cliff. Whoever survived today had a chance to survive the war because each day brought the end closer.

Wallenberg soon surprised his Budapest colleagues with his determination to issue as many *Schutzpässe* as possible. As diplomats they had other considerations. Was this correct procedure from a diplomatic point of view? Was it in line with foreign office policy? Would great numbers of passes produce an "inflation" and thus devalue the passes? According to Lars Berg, an attaché who served at the legation at that time, many hours were spent in painful discussion of these matters.

"But in the end Wallenberg always won," Berg reported in an interview in New York on February 14, 1980. "He won partly because he was so persistent, but finally because he had this very strong argument—it will save lives."

Wallenberg's normal intensity had undoubtedly been quickened by the fact that soon after his arrival, he received a complete copy of the "Auschwitz Protocols," which he had evidently not seen before leaving Stockholm. In his first report to the foreign office, on July 17, he sent an extract of some of the details from the document. He told about the crematoria working day and night. He wrote of the arrival at the camp of sixteen hundred French Aryans prominent in finance and politics, as well as noted journalists. He reported that they were brutally treated, some shot and the others later sent to Mauthausen. He added that Jews were arriving from France, Holland and Italy, in addition to the vast numbers from Hungary. He wrote about the biological experiments on both men and women, and the fact that Gypsies were also included. He wrote about the castration of men—and about the orchestra, which was forced to play lively waltzes to cover the screams of victims who were shot in groups of two hundred to three hundred, after having been forced to dig their own graves.

In that first communication to Stockholm he enclosed a note to his mother, asking her to invite Lauer to dinner and to tell him that his wife's family had been deported and probably all killed, including "the little child." He said, "I haven't the heart to tell him."

A few days after his arrival, Wallenberg was treated to a close-up view of the struggle he was facing. Eichmann had been enraged by the cancellation of the Budapest deportations and decided to show his power by deporting fifteen hundred Jews who were being held in internment camps just outside of Budapest. The group included prominent journalists and lawyers and people who had been arrested for "crimes" like not attaching their yellow stars properly. Most of the Jews were to come from the Kistarcsa camp. However, the Hungarian director of the camp tipped off Sándor Bródy, a representative of the Benevolent Society of Hungarian Jews, who made regular visits to the camp. Bródy at once contacted the Jewish Council. The council contacted Cardinal Serédi, the primate of Hungary; Vilmos Apor, the Protestant bishop of Hungary; all the neutral legations; and the regent's son.

Immediately, protests were sent to Horthy, who ordered Interior Minister Andor Jaross to halt the deportation. The train was already steaming toward the Hungarian border when Captain Leó Lullay, Ferenczy's deputy, caught up with it and brought it back.

Eichmann was now in a towering rage. According to Wisliceny's account, written after the war, he fumed, "Nothing like this has ever happened to me before." He devised a new plan.

He ordered the members of the Jewish Council to appear at his offices at Hotel Majestic on July 19 at 8 A.M. They appeared promptly and waited ... and waited. After a few hours SS *Haupsturmführer* Otto Hunsche entered and talked to them about improving the mood of the Jewish community. He asked why the Jews didn't go to the movies and other taunting questions. The council members recognized they were being detained for some sinister reason, but were unable to leave or make phone calls. They were held until 7:30 P.M. Then they learned that 1,220 of those set for the original transport had been loaded onto freight cars and deported. (Of the original group, 280 had been moved to a different prison at Sárvár and were, for the moment, saved.)

Horthy received strong protests from abroad. Minister of Finance Lajos Reményi-Schneller, who was acting as prime minister during Sztojay's illness, offered assurances that the deportation from Kistarcsa had been carried out without the knowledge or consent of the Hungarian government and that it would not be repeated, because the Hungarian government would take sole responsibility for the Jewish question in the future.

Nevertheless, only five days later it happened again. A German commando force overcame protesting Hungarian guards at the Sárvár camp and deported fifteen hundred internees.

These events convinced Wallenberg that he had to do something to afford additional protection for the people who held *Schutzpässe*. He wanted to acquire a group of special houses to be placed under Swedish protection, and this effort took him to Lieutenant Colonel László Ferenczy, the man who had so effectively carried out the deportations from the provinces.

The situation was grotesque, but Ferenczy now seemed eager to cooperate in any plan to save Jews. Officially, he was the liaison between the Eichmann *Sonderkommando* and the Hungarian authorities. The reason for his change of heart was not difficult to perceive. Suddenly he, like many other Nazis, began to feel that they were not on the winning side after all. The Allies were fanning out on the continent and the Russians steadily advancing from the East. Ferenczy saw that the chance of his hanging as a war criminal was increasing by the day. He had to do something to earn postwar credits with the Jews and their friends.

Since Wallenberg didn't speak Hungarian, he asked Mrs. Elizabeth Kasser, a volunteer worker for the Hungarian Red Cross, to serve as his interpreter. Mrs. Kasser's husband Alexander, general secretary of the Swedish Red Cross, came with them to see if he could gain some additional privileges for the Red Cross.

Thirty-six years after this visit Mrs. Kasser was able to recall Wallenberg's anger as the three of them were kept waiting for a long time in the anteroom in a huge, formidable-looking building filled with armed gendarmes.

"Finally Ferenczy came to us and made a long speech about how we should be ashamed of ourselves for helping Jews, and what awful people Jews are," remembered Mrs. Kasser. She added that she did not translate all the terrible things Ferenczy said because she was afraid that Wallenberg, already irritated, would lose his temper.

Nevertheless, in the end the visit was a success. Wallenberg got Ferenczy to agree to setting apart three houses under special Swedish protection, ostensibly for 650 people who were to emigrate to Sweden as soon as conditions permitted. Taking advantage of Ferenczy's generous mood, Alexander Kasser also asked that some houses be placed under Swedish Red Cross protection; this was also granted.

Mrs. Kasser recalled that after leaving the building, Wallenberg, who usually conducted himself with great seriousness and dignity, broke into a joyous jig.

"As soon as we were out of sight of that building, we put our arms around each other and did a sort of Indian dance in the street."

Mrs. Kasser was among the few in Budapest who was privileged to see Wallenberg's lighter side. His staff saw an intense, dedicated man who worked virtually round the clock (he allowed only four hours for sleep) and had not a second to spare for frivolity. "I never heard him utter an extra word," said Sándor Ardai, who served as his chauffeur for a time. Others noted that he seemed cold and taciturn, and those who failed in their responsibilities for any reason were aware of a fierce temper beneath the surface. Mrs. Kasser recalls his exploding when one individual who had been given a *Schutzpass* asked if he could use it to go to the theater. "You give a person a chance to live and rooms to live in and he wants to go to the theater! This will make an anti-Semite of me!" Wallenberg wound up laughing.

Kasser recalled that he asked Wallenberg whether something could be done to give some official approval to the letters of protection the Red Cross had been handing out to individuals who applied for help. He realized that there was absolutely nothing official behind the documents the Red Cross had been issuing:

Wallenberg said he agrees to do anything which helps people. He would try to cover for us, but he doesn't know how. He expects that there will be official resistance from the ambassador because if he knows about it he must forbid it. It may be a breach of international diplomatic rules. The ambassador may even have to report his official position back to Stockholm. But we shouldn't take that seriously, because if we would then we couldn't do anything. Wallenberg will explain his action after the war and Langlet will explain his. He is certain that when the truth will be known, the bureaucrats will find a way to justify it.

He went on to say that the times are such that nobody has the opportunity, the patience or the time to analyze what is illegal because everything that is being done by the Nazis in the name of the law is inhuman, unjust. Therefore whatever is illegal becomes legal. The main thing is to help.

Wallenberg's visit to Ferenczy marked the beginning of what came to be known as the international ghetto, an area in which people who were supposedly about to emigrate under Swedish, Swiss or Portuguese passports could live in houses protected by the neutral legations.

At that time Swiss Consul Charles Lutz, who had worked with Zionist official Miklós Krausz to secure top-level approval for the emigration of 7,000 Jews, opened the Glass House at 29 Vadász Street as an annex to the Swiss legation. It was called the Glass House because it had been turned over to the Swiss by Arthúr Weisz, a glass and ceramics manufacturer. It became a turbulent center in which thousands of desperate people daily cried, pleaded and offered everything they owned to be included on the list. The Swiss sponsored seven thousand special passports for people who would supposedly emigrate; they decided to interpret the seven thousand as applying to family heads, which would bring about forty thousand individuals under Swiss protection. In addition eight hundred passports had been issued under Swedish and War Refugee Board sponsorship. There was not much hope that emigration would be possible while the war was on, but the passports provided some temporary form of protection.

Unfortunately this Swiss "collective passport" proved to be a poor protection. It was much less impressive than the Swedish document. It was not signed by the Swiss ambassador and it did not carry the bearer's picture. But the house on Vadász Street became very important in the rescue operation because a troop of young Zionists moved in and set up headquarters, trying to help those with the courage to flee Budapest. They distributed as many documents as possible. They opened a virtual printing factory for forged documents of all kinds, from baptismal papers to the Swedish *Schutzpässe*, which were difficult to reproduce.

Wallenberg was aware of these forged Swedish documents and did not protest, according to Bruce Teicholz, a Polish refugee who was living in Budapest under false baptismal papers and working actively with the underground. He became a businessman in New York and was interviewed on January 22, 1981.

Teicholz thought that Wallenberg ought to know the Zionists were making the forgeries. He went to him and told him. Wallenberg simply nodded and said, "I know."

Obviously Wallenberg's point of view was diametrically opposed to diplomatic protocol. It is most unlikely that he told his colleagues he had given forged Swedish documents tacit approval. His view that everything done under the Nazis in Hungary was illegal, and whatever helped people should be regarded as legal, must have been highly irritating to diplomats trained to work within the letter of the law, and who were responsible to their chiefs in the foreign office. Nevertheless, Wallenberg was able to persuade Danielsson to go on signing *Schutzpässe*. Officially, the number given to Hungarian authorities was 4,500, but unofficially, he is believed to have issued 15,000 to 20,000.

Word of Wallenberg's generosity quickly got around in Budapest. People were still not certain of how much the document would help when it came to a showdown, but they had to try. They manufactured Swedish connections. A woman with a boyfriend in Sweden was claimed as his fiancé. Another woman, named Klein, got hold of a Stockholm phone book and wrote to all the Kleins in it, saying, "Your family in Budapest is in danger." She got a response from someone willing to vouch for her and her family. But soon the requirement for sponsorship in Sweden was waived. Applicants simply renounced their Hungarian citizenship and declared their wish to become Swedish citizens.

Wallenberg soon had to move his operation out of the legation building and rent two adjacent buildings, both of which quickly became just as busy as the old headquarters had been. He did not confine his activities to issuing *Schutzpässe*. He also set up two hospitals and a soup kitchen, and took forty physicians on his staff. Word of his zeal reached Stockholm. On August 10 Ivor Olsen wrote to WRB director John Pehle:

I get the impression indirectly that the Swedish Foreign Office is somewhat uneasy about Wallenberg's activities in Budapest and perhaps feel that he has jumped in with too big a splash. They would prefer, of course, to approach the Jewish problem in the finest traditions of European diplomacy, which wouldn't help too much. On the other hand, there is much to be said for moving around quietly on this type of work. In any case, I feel that Wallenberg is working like hell and doing some good, which is the measure.

The fact is that Wallenberg's example served to stir the Spanish and Portuguese legations to issue protective passports. Spain offered passports to a small number of Jews who could trace their ancestry to Spain and had kept some ties with that heritage. A proposal to admit five hundred children accompanied by fifty to seventy adults to Tangier, which was under Spanish occupation, was discussed at length, but fizzled in the face of the takeover by the Arrow Cross government in mid-October. The Portuguese issued more than seven hundred passports, but these carried little weight when the Arrow Cross took over.

On August 4, his thirty-second birthday, Wallenberg wrote to his mother:

I have organized a large office with 40 employees. We have rented two houses on each side of the legation and each section grows from day to day. My secretary, Countess Nákó, gave me a portfolio, an almanac, an inkstand, flowers and champagne for my birthday! I have rented a beautiful 18th century villa on a hill, from which the view is superb.

The gossip was that Wallenberg had a brief affair with "Countess" Nákó. Wallenberg's colleague, Lars Berg, was dubious.

Countess [everyone in Hungary was at least a baron] Elizabeth Nákó was a very capable and resourceful woman. She could procure almost anything—from whisky to Christmas trees—and was an excellent help to us all. She was very fat but with a pretty face and was constantly in good humor, even in the worst of circumstances. First she worked with Raoul Wallenberg, but later she came over to my B-Department as a secretary and my guardian angel. I believe she had some Jewish blood in her and in the end she moved over to my house to be protected from the Arrow Cross people. I was quite happy about it, as she managed my six "inherited" servants much better than I could do with my poor Hungarian.

While Wallenberg's operation instilled great hope in thousands of Jews, thousands more were increasingly panic-stricken and pessimistic. Many did not have the physical or psychological stamina to stand in the long lines waiting for a document. The fact that some Jews were to be ensconced in "protected" houses was highly disturbing to unprotected Jews. A blow that contributed to their panic was the disappearance on August 9 of Philip Freudiger, the leader of the Orthodox community of Pest, with his family and friends—seventy-two people in all. He had managed to bribe *Haupsturmführer* Wisliceny with boxes of bonbons. Inside some of the bonbons were jewels. Freudiger was considered to have intimate knowledge of what was going on in Hungarian-German relations. His escape by train to Bucharest spoke for itself.

In his report, written after the war, Freudiger did not allude to his own escape, but justified the dealings of the Jewish Council with the SS by pointing out that at least some lives were saved through payments. He pointed out that this was a legitimate means of trying to save a life, adding that although American Jews and Israelis find inspiration and pride in the fighters of the Warsaw ghetto, who held off the Germans for a full month, nothing was achieved by the uprising except additional deaths of Jews:

Those who fought were killed, and the others sent to their death. The few who escaped and joined the partisans could have done so just as well without the uprising.... As this shows, resistance or uprisings against a superior armed adversary does not pay, and it is questionable whether resistance should have been organized or furthered even if it had been possible. The negotiations with the SS and payments to them accomplished the following: close to 1,700 persons went to Bergen-Belsen and were eventually released to Switzerland; 16,000 were sent to Strasshof rather than to Auschwitz, and remained alive.

Freudiger also notes that if Joel Brand had returned from Istanbul with a successful deal, hundreds of thousands might have been rescued. However, by mid-July the Jewish community had given up all hope for the Jews-for-trucks deal. The entire story had been leaked to the British and American press. Instead of a way of saving Jews from the gas chambers, it was interpreted as a "monstrous offer" designed to split the Allies. The release of the story to the press indicated that, at the cost of Jewish lives, the Western Allies wanted to make a definite open statement that there would be no secret deals to turn against the Russians.

In spite of the fact that the Brand deal was off, discussion of some form of ransom continued for many months in Switzerland between various German representatives and Roswell D. McClelland, the WRB representative, and Saly Mayer, a Swiss businessman working on behalf of the American Joint Distribution Committee. The complex negotiations continued to the last month of the war—with little ultimate effect on the fate of the Budapest Jews. However, 318 individuals on the Kasztner train were sent from Bergen-Belsen to Switzerland on August 21 as a token of the seriousness of German intentions in the negotiations. (Himmler had ordered that 500 be released, but Eichmann got the number cut to 318.) The remainder of the group arrived in Switzerland on December 7.

Throughout the summer Horthy walked a tightrope between the pressures of the Germans and the promises he had made to the Allies that there would be no more deportations. After July 20 he still hoped to be able to make an armistice with Churchill and Roosevelt. However, he did not know how to get rid of the Germans. He had made a deal that had been approved by Hitler himself, on the advice of Veesenmayer and Foreign Affairs Minister Joachim von Ribbentrop. The deal involved the 7,800 Jews who were allowed to emigrate. In return, Horthy was to agree to allow resumption of the deportations. He stalled.

Eichmann had eagerly set August 5 as a date for the first roundup of Jews in Budapest, but Horthy threw a wrench into the plan by relieving his interior minister, Andor Jaross, of his duties, along with his henchmen László Endre and László Baky. They were in control of the gendarmerie. Without the gendarmerie there could be no deportations.

Eichmann and Veesenmayer continued to apply pressure. Eichmann encircled the city with SS detachments, threatened to use the SS to handle the deportations and asked for the Jews of districts 7, 8 and 9 in Pest. When he was refused by the new Interior Minister Miklós Bonczos, he asked for a mere ten thousand Jews. He didn't get them.

Veesenmayer, at Horthy's elbow, kept the regent reminded of his agreement. Horthy's newly organized Council of Ministers, from which the most extreme Nazi factions had been eliminated, came up with a compromise:

1. The Hungarians would deliver to the Germans fifty thousand to sixty thousand Jews identified as "Galician and infiltrated" (Austrian and Polish).

2. Jews in the labor-service units and their families would be placed in ghettos in the countryside.

3. Jews legally exempted from the anti-Jewish laws, and those given a special exemption by Horthy, were to be retained in the country. (Included in the legal exemptions were heroes of World War I with high decorations, their wives and children; widows and orphans of soldiers killed in the war; converts married to Christians; and Christian pastors, deacons and deaconesses of Jewish origin.)

On their side, the Germans were to agree that the "Jewish question" was solved. The *Sonderkommando* would be recalled, the Germans would refrain from unilateral deportations, the emigration of Jews sponsored by the Swiss government and the International Red Cross and Swedish Red Cross would be permitted, the deported Jews would remain alive and the property of the deported Jews would be recognized as part of the Hungarian national wealth, i.e., not robbed by the Germans, as had happened in the deportations in the countryside.

The Jewish leaders were alerted by Ferenczy to a new deportation date, August 25. The Jewish Council appealed to the neutrals, the Red Cross and the Vatican. Wallenberg organized a meeting at which the following appeal was to be presented to the prime minister:

The Envoys of the neutral States represented in Budapest have been acquainted with the fact that the deportation of the Jews is about to be accomplished. They all know what this means, even though it be described as "labour service."

Regardless of the fact that Hungary's reputation is suffering extensively under these schemes, it is the human duty of the representatives of the neutral countries to protest against these actions, which are opposed to all Christian and humane feelings. The representatives of the neutral powers herewith request the Hungarian Government to forbid these cruelties, which ought never to have been started. They hope that Hungary will return to its humane and chivalrous traditions, which, until now, have guaranteed its place among civilized nations.

Budapest, August 21st, 1944
sgd:

Angelo Rotta, Papal Nuncio   *Carl Ivan Danielsson, Swedish*
Carlos de Liz Texeira,   *Minister*
Portuguese Chargé d'Affaires   *Miguel Sans-Briz, Spanish*
Antoine J. Kilchmann, Swiss   *Chargé d'Affaires*
Chargé d'Affaires

The appeal worked. The deportations did not take place.

The intervention of the neutrals had come at the right moment. On August 24, Rumania, overrun by Soviet forces, had pulled out of the Axis Alliance, joined the Allies and declared war on Germany and Hungary. Germany now needed Hungary more than ever to allow escape routes and supply lines to the troops in the Balkans. Horthy let Veesenmayer know that he would not allow a deportation to Germany, but would transfer the Budapest Jews to the interior of Hungary, into large camps.

On the same day Himmler agreed that all deportations from Hungary were to be stopped. Defeated, Eichmann requested that the *Sonderkommando* be recalled since there was no job for them. Himmler obliged and rewarded Eichmann for his work in Hungary with the Iron Cross Second Class. Eichmann retreated with Endre to the latter's country estate on the Austro-Hungarian border.

On August 29, Horthy found the courage to do what he had been wanting to do for a long time. He appointed General Géza Lakatos, the former commander of the First Hungarian Army, as prime minister. A new government was formed, excluding most of the extreme Nazi faction and including some latent anti-Nazis. However, the government remained in the difficult position of still being in the Axis but struggling to get out of the war. The Germans (even without Eichmann) kept pressing for "resettlement" of Jews into the countryside and the need for Jews for labor. The Jewish leaders were convinced that "resettlement" was a step toward deportation or destruction of the camps by Nazi bombs. The *Sonderkommando* had not actually been fully dissolved, and one of Eichmann's closest long-term associates, SS *Hauptsturmführer* Theodor Dannecker, remained in Budapest. Veesenmayer remained there too, still at Horthy's elbow.

Throughout the summer of 1944 the Allies forged ahead brilliantly. The Western Allies swept through Normandy and Brittany, and on August 25 Paris was liberated. General Patton pushed into Southwest France, General Hodge's forces were moving swiftly up through Italy, and the Soviet forces advanced through the Carpathian Mountains north of Hungary. Rumania, having joined the Allies, added its forces to the Russians moving to the border of Hungary.

The critical military situation did not prevent the Germans from concentrating on disposing of the Jews in one way or another. Veesenmayer bargained for all able-bodied Jews to be put in labor camps in the provinces. Children, the old and those unfit for labor would be placed in two other camps. The International Red Cross was delegated to find acceptable campsites, but in the entire month of September no acceptable site was found.

Ferenczy had secret meetings with members of the Jewish Council and Hungarian labor leaders to organize resistance against the Germans. Ferenczy had to use his contacts with Jewish leaders to win an audience with the regent. He informed Horthy about German troop strength in the country. Petö discussed all developments with Horthy, Jr.

It was an exceptionally bright and beautiful early fall in Budapest, and the Jews were suddenly hopeful that the war would end soon. They were given freedom of movement during the high holy days. They began to make jokes. A popular one making the rounds was that a bearded, religious Jew was seen in the streets, brandishing his Swedish papers, telling an SS man to treat a Swedish citizen with respect.

From her cell in Pest County jail, Hannah Szenes was giving Hebrew lessons and lectures on Zionism. Her mother was told that she would probably soon be released.

Horthy finally came to face the fact that the Western Allies were not going to enter the Balkans. They were going to let the Soviet Union dominate East Europe. If he wanted to get out of the war he would have to make an armistice with the Russians. He sent representatives to the Russians to discuss terms.

On September 29, Wallenberg triumphantly reported to the foreign office that "The agreement reached between the Hungarians and the Germans that all Jews were to be evacuated from Budapest to the countryside outside the capital has been completely sabotaged by the Hungarian authorities and has not yet resulted in a single Jew leaving Budapest." However, he noted that the Germans were making threatening gestures like concentrating SS units in the capital.

He reported that he was winding down the work of his department and now had only one hundred employees, and that forty more would soon leave. The holders of Swedish passports who had been drafted for labor service were about to be released and there would be a general release of internees. That, he said modestly, was the result of "the work of this department."

The same day he wrote to Lauer:

I am going to do everything possible to get home soon, but you must understand that such a big organization cannot be wound up easily. The moment the occupation [Russian] is accomplished this organization will cease to function. Until then, though, the work of our organization will remain necessary. It would be very hard just to stop it. I will try to get home a few days before the Russians arrive.

On October 12 he reported to Stockholm:

The Russian advance has increased the hope of the Jews that their unfortunate plight will soon be ended. Many have of their own accord already ceased wearing the Star of David. Their fears that the Germans might at the last moment carry out a pogrom still remain, however, despite the fact that there are no positive signs that any such happening will occur.

In what was apparently intended as his farewell to his mission in Budapest, he wrote the following letter to Ivor Olsen:

When I now look back on the three months I have spent here I can only say that it has been a most interesting experience, and I believe not without results. When I arrived the situation of the Jews was very bad indeed. The development of military events and a natural psychological reaction among the Hungarian people have changed many things. We at the Swedish legation have perhaps only been an instrument to convert this outside influence into action in the various government offices. I have taken quite a strong line in this respect, although of course I have had to keep within the limits assigned to me as a neutral.

It has been my object all the time to try to help all Jews. This, however, could only be achieved by helping a whole group of Jews to get rid of their stars. I have worked on the hypothesis that those who were no longer under the obligation to wear the star would help their fellow-

sufferers. Also I have carried out a great deal of enlightenment work among the key men in charge of Jewish questions here. I am quite sure that our activity—and that means in the last instance yours—is responsible for the freeing at this time of the interned Jews. These numbered many hundreds....

Mr. Olsen, believe me, your donation in behalf of the Hungarian Jews has done an enormous amount of good. I think that they will have every reason to thank you for having initiated and supported the Swedish Jewish action the way you have in such a splendid manner.

On Sunday morning, October 15, the sun sparkled on the Danube. At 1 P.M. a proclamation from the regent was read on the radio that the war, into which Hungary had been dragged by the Germans, was lost. He blamed all the horrors of the preceding months on the Gestapo and the SS. Then the Order of the Day was addressed to the Armed Forces. Horthy called upon them to remain loyal to their oaths and to follow his instructions.

The war was over! In the labor battalions the men threw away their picks and shovels, and in Budapest Jews tore off their yellow stars and rushed into the street and danced. They could rejoin the living.

Not yet.

EIGHT
INFERNO

The regent's armistice proclamation was broadcast twice. Then dead silence. Suddenly there was the sound of martial music—German marches. An announcer came on the air stating in a flat tone that the fighting would continue. More martial music. People were bewildered.

That evening it was announced that the Hungarian Nazi *Nyilas* Party—the Arrow Cross—was in power, and that Ferenc Szálasi would lead the nation in continued warfare.

What had gone wrong? Everything. The Germans had many informants inside the government and closely followed all the regent's moves. They had long watched Horthy, Jr.'s, meetings with Jewish and resistance leaders. Ferenczy had kept himself covered on both flanks. He plotted with the Jews and other anti-Germans, and kept the Germans informed about what was going on.

The Germans had worked out a complete plan with the Hungarian Nazis for a *Nyilas* takeover. SS *Obergruppenführer* Erich von dem Bach-Zelewski, chief of the anti-Partisan units, had been called from Warsaw to deal with potential trouble in Budapest. Colonel Otto Skorzeny, Himmler's daring commando fighter, who the year before had rescued Mussolini from a remote hilltop in the Apennines, was called into Budapest to handle Horthy, Jr. The regent's son was tricked into a meeting with individuals he believed represented Tito's partisans. He was seized, wounded when he tried to get away, covered with a blanket and dragged into a car. While the armistice proclamation was being read on the radio, the aged regent was already meeting with Hitler's special envoy, Rudolf Rahn.

Horthy was informed that his only remaining son was in German hands. (His older son, István, whom he had hoped to make his heir as regent, had been killed in 1942 piloting a plane on the Russian front.) Horthy was further informed that the city was surrounded by four German divisions, and that two German Tiger tanks stood on his lawn with guns pointed at the palace windows. The Germans were arming the Arrow Cross and had seized the radio station. *Panzerfaust* (Armored Fist), as the entire operation was called, was a complete success.

Broken, the regent informed Lakatos that he was willing to step down. All he wanted was his son and the opportunity to take some of his personal belongings from the palace. The Germans and Arrow Cross got to work looting the palace, but the Germans would not let the Hungarians keep the loot. General Lakatos was hustled into a bathroom of the palace by German guards. There the agreement turning over the reins of the government to Szalasi was signed. The regent's twenty-year reign came to an end. Horthy was escorted into exile in Germany the next day, but his son was deported to Mauthausen. He was later transferred to Dachau and was liberated there by American troops in the last days of the war.

Pandemonium instantly broke out. The Russians were advancing steadily from the East, Budapest was under almost constant bombardment and the radio blared continual terrifying warnings of the "Jewish-Bolshevik" menace. Wild rumors were circulating that the Jews were signaling the bombers, which were unleashing explosive toys to be picked up by children. Throughout the country there were attacks on the Jews in labor-service companies, and in one small town, Pusztavam, a company of 160 doctors, engineers and other professionals was wiped out.

In Budapest, Arrow Cross bands, including young teenagers wearing death's-head armbands and armed with automatic rifles, machine guns and grenades, ran through the streets looting and shooting Jews. The macabre figure of a black-robed priest, Father András Kun, bearing a huge crucifix, a revolver and hate pamphlets, appeared in the streets at the head of bands which brought Jews to torture houses for a going-over before they were dragged to be shot into the Danube. A game was invented—strip the Jews naked, tie three together, shoot the middle one at close range and watch the weight of his body drag the other two into the river. There was a new wave of Jewish suicides.

The next afternoon houses marked with the yellow star were ordered locked for ten days. Nobody could go in or out. Doctors could not tend the sick. The dead could not be buried. Nobody could shop for food.

Eichmann returned to the city. He brought a plan for completing the job of dejewifying Hungary.

The high morale Wallenberg had instilled in his staff broke down. Only a handful turned up for work the following day. Some went into hiding for the remainder of the war.

Jews in hiding usually stayed with Christian friends or relatives, but they knew they endangered their protectors. Many compassionate Christians were turned in by neighbors and met the same fate as Jews. Some in hiding slept in different places every night. Some walked the streets or rode the streetcars all day, turning in another direction or getting off the car if they noted a nearby Gestapo or SS man or heard the yells of a *Nyilas* band. Others never left the house.

The day after the coup a small desperate band of Jewish laborers, joined by a handful of Socialists and Communists, got hold of a cache of arms and attempted an insurrection in Teleki Square in the heart of the ghetto. Immediately a large force of SS men and Hungarian police sped to the spot, emptied all the houses around the square and conducted a mass execution. Within hours the square was strewn with hundreds of bodies.

This was followed by a mass roundup. Some six thousand Jews, including Chief Rabbi Ferenc Hevesi and other leading members of the community, were herded into the large synagogues on Dohány Street and Rumbach Sebestyén Street. They were held for several days without food, water or any facilities, and were packed so closely that there was no way to separate the dead and the dying.

Wallenberg and Charles Lutz, the Swiss chargé d'affaires, went to the synagogue and managed to secure the release of hundreds who held Swedish and Swiss protection documents. Later protests by the Papal Nuncio and other prominent Hungarians finally brought about the release of the remainder of the hostages.

The new *Nyilas* government evidently felt the need to make a gesture toward containing the anarchy that had erupted by promising to accomplish the same ends officially. The following pronouncement on the fate of the Jews was offered by the new minister of the interior, Gábor Vajna, on October 18:

In connection with the Jewish question which in recent months has given rise to so much excitement among both the Jews and certain

*circles of their friends, I declare that we shall solve it. This solution—
even if ruthless—will be what the Jews deserve by reason of their previous
and present conduct. To solve the Jewish question, detailed regulations
will be published and carried out. Let no one be an arbitrary or self-
appointed judge of the Jews, because the solution of this question is the
task of the state. And this question—everyone may rest assured—we
shall solve. Let me emphatically warn the Jews and those serving their
interests that all the organs of state power are vigilantly watching their
conduct, and that I shall execute with particular severity the regulations
in effect and still to be issued, in view of the war. In this connection I do
not recognize Jews as belonging to the Roman Catholic, Lutheran or
Israelite denominations but only as persons of the Jewish race.* I
recognize no letter of safe-conduct of any kind nor any foreign passport
which a Jew of Hungarian nationality may have received from whatever
source or person.

The last pronouncement meant the end of the protection
afforded by the *Schutzpässe.*

Fortunately, Wallenberg had managed to socialize sufficiently to
have met Baroness Gábor Kemény, a young woman of Austrian background married to the new Nazi minister for foreign affairs.

He went to urge her to prevail on her husband to see that the
order regarding the exceptional cases, those holding foreign passports,
be rescinded. The baroness was pregnant with her first child, and he
warned her that from the way the war was going, there was a good
chance that the father of her child would be hung as a war criminal. On
the other hand, if the minister could show that he had tried to alleviate
the harsh policies of the government, he had a chance of getting off.

Further, Wallenberg had another card to play. Stockholm had
not recognized the Arrow Cross government. If Kemény could see to it
that the diplomatic passports of the neutrals would be recognized,
Wallenberg would do what he could to help get recognition for the
Szálasi government.

It worked. Wallenberg had asked that announcement of the
new regulations be made over the radio by Kemény himself, the way
Vajna had made his pronouncement. The Baroness accompanied her
husband to the radio studio to make sure that he made the announcement. The new ruling applied to Jews protected by the other neutral
powers as well.

(The baroness shortly afterward left war-torn Budapest for Italy, and Wallenberg, with appropriate chivalry and diplomatic fanfare, came to the station to see her off with a bouquet of roses. However, the Swedish government refused to recognize the Szálasi regime. The baron was hanged as a war criminal along with all of Szálasi's cohorts after a trial by the People's Court at the end of the war.)

Wallenberg's ability to maintain the fiction of special immunity for the people under his protection was almost miraculous in view of the fact that both Eichmann and the new government became more determined to finish off the Budapest Jews each day the Red Armies drew closer.

Wallenberg kept expanding the number of *Schutzpässe* he issued. He needed help in getting portrait photos, and Tom Veres volunteered to work for him. He asked Tom whether it would be possible to take photos from a hidden camera. Tom devised the trick of hiding his camera in his shawl. Thereafter he accompanied Wallenberg on many rescue missions, taking hundreds of pictures of detention and deportation centers. Wallenberg clearly wanted the world to see and know as much of the Nazi horror as possible and viewed this as part of his work in Budapest.

Five days after the Szálasi government took over, Arrow Cross gangs and police barged into the yellow-star houses and pulled out men between ages sixteen and sixty. The ill and physically handicapped were not excluded, nor were those with foreign documents. They were dragged into courtyards at rifle point, beaten, kicked, robbed of valuables and taken to large open spaces where they were formed into companies and sent to the outskirts of Budapest to dig trenches. Many were so badly abused that they died before they got to a labor company. Some were shot in the street. Others managed to escape or bribe their way out.

Women did not fare much better. Women between eighteen and forty, except those who were pregnant or had infants, were hauled out for labor service, cleaning rubble. Seamstresses were called upon to sew sheets together. These were used to package the huge quantities of goods appropriated from Jews. Big trainloads of these packages were sent into Austria, where they were found at railroad stations when the Allies marched in.

Hannah Szenes, the young Zionist paratrooper, was removed from Conti Street prison to a military jail where, on October 28, she was tried for treason before a military court. There was no one to defend her. She offered her own statement. No record was kept, but witnesses— including Nazi guards—were so moved they were able to piece together what she said for her mother.

She denied the treason charge and accused her accusers of treason by joining with Hungary's enemies, the Germans. She said she had grown up loving her country and caring deeply about the sufferings of the Hungarian people. Her father, a Hungarian author, taught her to have faith in the good. But she had been cancelled out as a citizen of Hungary by Jew haters. She had found a new spiritual homeland in Eretz Israel. But she still sympathized with the Hungarian people. She implored her judges to turn against the leaders who had brought disaster to the country. She called upon them to "save my people." She refused to ask the court for mercy.

The bright weather of early fall underwent a sudden change. An exceptionally cold and rainy season began. On November 2, during a driving rain, the Soviet troops broke through the German and Hungarian forces defending the outskirts of the capital. There was a disorderly retreat. The Jewish labor-service men, starving and forced to carry heavy equipment, sloshed through the mud and rain. They were beaten with rifle butts if they did not keep up, and shot when they fell helplessly into the mud. There were thousands of deaths as the defenders retreated to retrench their lines in the south and southeastern areas of the city. *Nyilas* bands shot at the labor-service men for sport as they attempted to cross the Horthy Miklós Bridge over the Danube. Things got so bad that the Budapest police were called out to stop them.

Early in the cold and foggy morning of November 7, Hannah Szenes was taken out of her cell in the military jail and told she had been found guilty. She was executed in the prison yard by an Arrow Cross squad. She refused to be blindfolded.

Hannah's mother was told what had happened when she arrived at the jail with a food package. She had been advised a week earlier that she ought to get a lawyer, somebody influential, for her daughter. She had wandered about the mad, bomb-shattered city ducking air raids and *Nyilas* gangs, seeking Kasztner. She was unable to get to him or anybody else of importance.

The following night Katherine Szenes was among thousands of women herded out of their homes into the brickyard at Óbuda, on the outskirts of the city. The group was the first in a series of "death marches," deportations on foot to Hegyeshalom, 125 miles away on the Austrian border. They were to be used to build fortifications.

The group was composed mainly of women, young boys and older men. The younger men were already in the labor service companies. The women had suddenly been pulled out of their homes or picked up on the streets. Most wore light clothing and many had on high heels. They were not provided with any coverings and were forced to march, driven by the rifle butts of Hungarian soldiers, for a week on virtually no food. They slept in open fields or primitive shelters without walls, or on barges along the Danube. Thousands died along the way either by giving up, lying down in ditches and allowing themselves to be shot, or by throwing themselves from the barges into the icy waters of the Danube.

The death marches were so macabre that even a Nazi general, Hans Jüttner, making an official tour of inspection of the Waffen-SS divisions in the area, found the sight of the marchers and those lying helplessly in ditches along the road, mostly women, so "truly terrifying" that he inquired who was responsible for the march. He was told it was *Obersturmbannführer* Eichmann.

Wallenberg, Lutz, representatives of the International Red Cross and the Papal Nuncio, as well as some Christian physicians, brought soup and medical aid to the suffering thousands. Their supplies were pitifully inadequate. They managed to rescue hundreds who had protection passes when they visited the detention centers at which people were assembled before they were taken off on the marches. Sometimes they managed to rescue some along the line of the march. At the Eichmann trial in Jerusalem in 1961, Aryeh Breslauer reported that Wallenberg sent him to the border with a typewriter and hundreds of blank immunity passes. He was able to fill in hundreds of these blanks. He testified that the individuals who got them were brought back to Budapest.

It may be that some of this rescue work was made possible by the fact that the "workers" arrived at Hegyeshalom in such hopeless condition that no use could be made of them. There were epidemics of dysentery and typhoid at the camp.

According to Wallenberg's colleague Per Anger, who accompanied him on some of his trips, Eichmann himself presided over a special SS unit at Hegyeshalom. There the half-dead arrivals were counted off like cattle: "Four hundred and eighty-nine—check!"

(*"Vierhundert-neunundachtzig—stimmt gut!"*) The Hungarian officer received a receipt that said everything was in proper order. Anger reports that Wallenberg initiated checkpoints along the roads leaving Budapest and at the border station to stop the deportations of those holding protective passports.

Wallenberg again and again made excursions to the detention centers and appeared along the route of the march, pulling out people with protection papers and bringing medical aid and hot soup. He also went on the "death ships," barges tied up along the Danube where the marchers were sometimes forced to spend the night. He brought medicines and words of comfort.

The effect of Wallenberg's presence on a group assembled one night at the Obuda brickworks just outside Budapest is best described by Susan Tabor, who is today a librarian at the Hebrew Union College in New York. Mrs. Tabor had been seized with her mother. Her father and husband were both with labor service companies:

When we reached the outskirts of the city, we were herded into a brick factory. There were holes in the floor, which could not be seen in the darkness. Some people fell and were trampled over because the guards hurried us mercilessly into the building. Once we were all in, there was hardly room on the floor for everybody to sit. There was no light, no water, no food, no doctors, no first aid, no sanitary facilities, no one was allowed outside. Armed Nazis walked around stepping on people, abusing them, cursing and shooting. We were beaten. Our spirit was broken. Somehow the night passed. The next morning we were supposed to continue the march towards Austria, but hours passed and nothing was happening.

Then suddenly at one end of the building we saw people in civilian clothes with a loudspeaker and flashlights—and there was Raoul Wallenberg. We just stared at him, not even realizing that he was talking to us, not even comprehending what he was saying. He was telling us that he demanded that those with Schutzpässe should be allowed to return to Budapest. He further informed us that medical doctors and nurses had volunteered to come in, to take care of the sick and wounded; he demanded that outhouses be provided.

Not long after, two doctors and nurses came with some medical supplies. They announced that they would try to see those most urgently

*needing help if the neighbors of those people would guide them.
Somehow those beaten people straightened their backs, and from every
corner you could hear,* "Shema Yisrael, Adonai eloheinu, Adonai
echad." *(The Hebrew chant of faith—"Hear O Israel, the Lord is our God,
the Lord is one.)*

To Mrs. Tabor this burst into the ancient chant meant that some
were given hope, some getting ready for death with dignity. ("It
happened because we saw that someone cared, someone thought we
were human beings worth saving.")

Mrs. Tabor and her mother removed their yellow stars and
escaped in the dark. They hid with gentile friends until the end of the
war. They were reunited with their husbands and emigrated to the
United States after the war.

When the death marches were brought to a halt at the end of
November, deportations by rail were resumed. These usually involved
men pulled out of the labor service companies, to be shipped for labor
in the Reich, replacing the worn-out and discarded bodies.

Wallenberg made dramatic appearances at the train stations
when a deportation was set. He loped in, dressed in his worn raincoat
with his broad-brimmed Anthony Eden hat, an entourage of his staff
behind him. He then proceeded to take a highly "legalistic" position. He
created an office at the station by calmly opening a folding table and
settling down with his big notebook. He then demanded that those with
Swedish *Schutzpässe* come forward. He solemnly checked off their
names in his big book and separated them from the others. Then he
asked for those with preliminary application papers. Some immediately
caught on to the fact that any piece of paper would do. His errand boy,
Jonny Moser, at that time eighteen, remembers running among the men,
encouraging them to step forward. Wallenberg's photographer, Tom, was
standing by fiddling with his shawl, secretly taking picutres.

All the time the *Nyilas* guards stood watching. They were under
orders to cooperate. The *Nyilas* government still hoped for recognition
by Sweden. The only time shots were fired was when Wallenberg
climbed onto the roof of a train and distributed passes to all the hands
that could reach him through an opening. Then warning shots were
aimed above his head.

At the same time, Wallenberg was barraging the Ministry of
Foreign Affairs with memoranda protesting atrocities. The Arrow Cross

responded by demanding that the thousands under foreign protection leave the country. If they did not, they would be subject to deportation. Of course, it was impossible to move anybody at that time except for military purposes.

Wallenberg decided to call their bluff. He presented a memorandum posing a series of hopeless questions: How soon after the departure of the first convoy to their destination should the second convoy be prepared to leave? Should the potential travelers report to their local authorities? Did they need permission to take food for the long journey? The Hungarian authorities were stumped and didn't reply. The next time they demanded that the Swedish-protected Jews leave, Wallenberg pointed to the unanswered questions.

In mid-November some 15,600 "protected" Jews were forced to move to yellow-star houses. There they were constantly harassed by *Nyilas* raiding parties, supposedly making a check of protective passes, but actually bent on robbery. Nevertheless, people felt safer in the thirty-two Swedish buildings and seventy-two Swiss buildings, which quickly became filled with illegal residents.

As Wallenberg's name became legendary, more and more people came to him with individual crises. One night a member of his staff, Tibor Vándor, came with his wife, who was in labor. No hospital would admit her. Wallenberg gave up his apartment and got a physician for her. In the morning he was named godfather of a baby girl. He named her Yvonne Nina Maria, after his sister and aunt.

Another night Klari Rajk, a woman he had never seen before and who had no protection documents, came to him at 4 A.M. Her husband had been able to avoid labor service because he was a World War I hero with a very high decoration. But now he had been seized and was about to be deported from the Josefváros Station. She found out where Wallenberg was living and went to his apartment.

He dressed immediately and we drove to the station. Along the way he took all the details about my husband and filled out a Swedish passport for him. He went up to the Nyilas guards and showed them the passport. The guard went to the car where my husband was and called his name and he came out. The three of us left the station and returned to Wallenberg's flat. Then he settled us in a Swedish protected house at 1 Jokai Street.

This house was raided and most of the inhabitants killed on January 8, but Mrs. Rajk, her husband and twelve-year-old son managed to escape; after the war they emigrated to Israel.

Dr. George Basyai of Munich remembers standing at the Ferencvarosi Palyaudvar freight railway station one night in December, awaiting deportation.

Suddenly a group of men came and said, "Those with Swedish passports should form a line."... My brother had such a passport, but I did not. My brother refused to move to that line without me. But then a very good friend, Laci Geiger, who was among the Swedish staff, detected me and my problem. He went to a man standing fifty yards from us and spoke to him. This man, I found out later, was Raoul Wallenberg. He came to us, led me to the people inspecting passports and was standing next to me until the Nazi commander inspected our documents. Mr. Wallenberg vouched for me so that I was able to join the group.

On December 9 the Red Army launched a massive offensive and reached the Danube at Vác, just north of Budapest. Marshal Rodion Malinovsky was moving from the east and Marshal Fyodor I. Tolbukhin was coming up from the south. The only exit from the city was to the west. The siege of Budapest had begun.

At the beginning of December all unprotected Jews were ordered to move to an overcrowded ghetto. By December 10 the ghetto was to be sealed behind tall wooden gates. The government maintained that with the Russians at the gates of the city the Jews might start an uprising. Pessimists had another interpretation—a Nazi pogrom was planned before the Russians could get inside the city.

The Szálasi government was forced to move to Sopron in the west of Hungary, near the Austrian border. In the midst of this crisis situation, before leaving, Interior Minister Gábor Vajna took the trouble to issue an edict: All the streets, squares and roads in the city named after Jews or individuals with Jewish connections were to be renamed.

The day before the siege began, Wallenberg wrote a full report for his office in Stockholm, mentioning that he was inoculating his charges against typhoid, paratyphoid and cholera, that he now had 335 on staff plus 40 doctors and house wardens. These employees and their families were living in ten houses designated as belonging to the

embassy. He noted that the food shortage would soon be "catastrophic."
He reported, "As far as can be ascertained only ten Jews with Swedish
safe-conducts have up to now been shot in and around Budapest."
Wallenberg managed to get out this report along with pictures by
courier. He also sent a last letter to his mother:

Dearest Mother,
  I really don't know when I shall be able to stop feeling guilty.
Today there is another courier leaving and again I can only send you a
few hastily written lines.
  The situation is exciting and adventurous; my work load is
almost inhuman. Bandits are skulking around the city beating, looting
and shooting people. Among my staff I have already had 40 cases of
people being carried off and abused. All in all, however, we are in good
spirits and enjoy the battle....
  We hear the thundering cannons of the approaching Russians
day and night. Diplomatic duties have been intensified since the arrival
of Szálasi. I am almost single-handedly representing our legation at the
government offices. I have now met about ten times with the Foreign
Minister; twice with the acting Prime Minister, once with the Finance
Minister, etc....
  I have been well acquainted with the wife of the Foreign
Minister. Unfortunately, she has gone off to Merano [Italy].
  There is a great food shortage in Budapest. But we laid in a
good supply in time. I suspect that after the occupation it will be difficult
to return home so that I believe I will not get to Stockholm until about
Easter. But that is, after all, off in the future. At this point no one knows
yet what the occupation will bring. I will certainly try to return home as
quickly as possible.
  Today is really no time to make plans. I had thought certainly
to be with you for Christmas. But I must send you my Christmas
greetings and at the same time my good wishes for the New Year in this
way. Hopefully, the longed-for peace will soon be here.
  Dearest Mother, I am also enclosing two photographs which
were taken recently. You can see me at my desk surrounded by my
colleagues and employees.
  With all the work, time passes quickly, and I am frequently
invited to dinners at which we have suckling pig and other Hungarian
specialties.

Dearest Mother, I shall say farewell for today since the courier pouch must be made ready. I greet you and kiss you and the entire family warmly and deeply.

Your,
Raoul

In Swedish by hand, at the bottom of the page, he added, "My kisses also to Nina and the little girl." (Nina had given birth to a daughter in October.) And at the side of the page in Swedish he wrote, "Happy birthday—which is not far off."

Although Eichmann had to be fully aware of all of Wallenberg's activities, the two adversaries are known to have been in direct contact on only one occasion. It was a week or ten days before Christmas, according to Lars Berg, Wallenberg's colleague who played host at a dinner party for Eichmann.

Wallenberg had invited Eichmann to his apartment, but evidently had been so busy he had forgotten the invitation. Eichmann and his aide, both in full Nazi regalia, arrived at dinner time. Completely unprepared, Wallenberg phoned Berg. He knew Berg had an excellent cook who kept a fine larder. Berg said he was glad to help out, and they quickly repaired to his apartment.

The meal proved more than satisfactory. Over after-dinner brandy, Wallenberg initiated a discussion of Nazism with Eichmann. Wallenberg's impassioned, dazzling reasoning, geared to persuading cultivated friends, hardheaded businessmen and stubborn diplomats probably exhausted Eichmann, the obsessed Jew killer. Eichmann was not stupid, but he was not accustomed to intellectual discourse about Nazism.

Evidently he was at a loss for words. He finally said he never really believed in Nazism, but his role in the SS had given him power, the opportunity to enjoy beautiful women and high living (he is known to have had at least two mistresses in Budapest), and he wasn't planning to give these up.

Wallenberg pointed to the Russian artillery fire they could see from the windows of Berg's apartment and suggested that Eichmann didn't have much longer to enjoy his present life. Eichmann argued back that the war wasn't over yet. The Führer had not yet unleashed his secret weapons. The tide would turn.

"If it doesn't? Well, I'll hang, but I'll stick to my job to the end. As for you, Mr. Diplomat, don't think your diplomatic immunity will protect you forever. Accidents happen, you know." Eichmann rose, clicked his heels, bowed, thanked his host and left.

By this time Wallenberg was well aware of the possibility of an "accident." He slept at different apartments every night. The overt threat coming directly from Eichmann meant he had to be on guard at all times.

At the time he issued the dinner invitation Wallenberg undoubtedly had some hope of persuading Eichmann to stave off the final massacre of Jews in Budapest. However, Eichmann knew that he was among the top war criminals. There was no possibility of clemency for him. He was determined to go ahead with the Final Solution in Budapest.

And Wallenberg was determined to stop him.

NINE

HOLY NIGHT

On December 23 the bursts of Russian artillery fire began as usual at dawn and continued throughout the day. The Russians were gradually closing a huge iron band around the city. Waves of bombers roared toward the city at regular intervals, dropped their loads and roared away, leaving behind a few more shattered buildings and some fires. Night came, filled with stars. But again came the drone of bombers, and soon the stars were dimmed by searchlights scanning the sky and the flash of antiaircraft. Occasionally a hit plane burst into flame and spiraled to the ground like a huge, crazed comet.

That night Eichmann came to the Jewish Council headquarters on Síp Street, along with two of his henchmen. He had been drinking. His eyes were bloodshot and he was in one of his shouting rages. He demanded that the members of the Jewish Council appear at once. The trembling porter said he didn't know where to find them. Eichmann screamed that a telephone call had been made earlier to have them there at nine o'clock. The porter said he thought the order was for nine in the morning. He didn't know where he could find all the council members now. Eichmann told him to have them there the next morning or face the consequences. One of the henchmen then hit the porter repeatedly on the head with his pistol, leaving him bleeding and half conscious on the floor.

Eichmann did not keep the appointment the next morning. He left Budapest that day through the last remaining escape gap, two days before the Russians closed the ring around the city.

The members of the Jewish Council were certain that Eichmann had decided to finish them off that night, as a last symbolic gesture before leaving the city. He had been frustrated in his will to wipe out the Budapest Jews. This job would have climaxed his masterpiece— the lightning destruction of Hungarian Jewry. But Eichmann was no longer needed for the task. The blood lust of the Hungarian anti- Semites was at fever pitch. Perpetual fire from the Russians seemed to fan it. They believed the Jews were signaling the Russians.

Some six thousand Jewish children were living outside the ghetto under the protection of the International Red Cross. However, the *Nyilas* had been demanding for weeks that these children be brought into the ghetto. The Jewish Council kept stalling, but on December 12 five hundred children were brought in to one of the municipal schools in the ghetto. Conditions were so terrible that a protest by Hans Weyermann, Red Cross director and a Lutheran pastor, brought about a suspension of further transfers until December 22. On December 20 Wallenberg met with the Apostolic Nuncio and with Harald Feller, the Swiss chargé; Joseph Perlasca, the Spanish chargé; Count Pongros, the Portuguese chargé; and Swedish Minister Danielsson to draft a joint appeal to the Hungarian government:

The undersigned representatives of the neutral powers accredited to the Royal Hungarian Government have already twice respectfully requested the Royal Hungarian Government to intervene in favor of the per- secuted and outlawed Jews. Now that the Royal Hungarian Government have found it necessary—for reasons which need not be discussed here—to lock up the Jews in a ghetto, the representatives of the neutral powers undertake another diplomatic action in asking the Government to exempt from this order at least the children.

It would indeed be impossible to understand why innocents are to be punished or why measures of self-defence be taken against creatures absolutely incapable of doing any harm. Even admitting that the Royal Hungarian Government must protect itself against the possibility of disturbances, it is impossible to understand this continual fear of children. We have heard it said that the Jews are the enemies of Hungary, yet even in war conscience and the law condemn hostile actions against children. Why, therefore, force these innocent creatures to live in places in many respects resembling prisons and where the poor mites will see nothing but misery, pain and the desperation of old men and women also persecuted only on account of their race and origin. Every civilized nation respects children and the whole world will be painfully surprised should the traditionally Christian and gallant Hungary decide to institute steps against the innocent little ones.

This was the third and last joint appeal signed by the Nuncio and the three neutral representatives. Wallenberg had initiated the appeal and drafted it, but he was by no means confident that it would work. The desire of the *Nyilas* to get the children into the ghetto was terrifying. They were capable of anything. But the appeal reached them before Christmas Eve. If the children were left where they were for another day or so, then the Russians would be in the city, and it would all be over.... Late in the afternoon Wallenberg sat at his desk in the cellar at Üllöi Street trying to conquer fatigue and go over the reports of the day, trying to determine where food and medicines were most needed and what new emergencies seemed to be developing. There was a sound at the door.

"Merry Christmas!"

He looked up to see Elizabeth Kasser, smiling, radiating warmth and hopefulness, just as she had on the day they had gone together to see Ferenczy to negotiate for the Swedish houses.

"Merry Christmas!" He rose from his desk for a holiday greeting and Mrs. Kasser thrust a small but heavy package into his hands.

"But please, no presents..."

"Open it, please," insisted Mrs. Kasser.

He tore open the wrappings to find a small, exquisite statue, a Pallas Athena, goddess of wisdom. He gasped.

"It's genuine, authenticated by the Athens Museum," said Mrs. Kasser, pointing to the small mark at the base. "We bought it on our honeymoon."

Wallenberg turned the statue around, admiring its delicacy and grace from every angle. It was the one miracle that could suddenly wash away his fatigue and the unceasing images of brutality and suffering that had been with him for the past months. Athena—beauty and wisdom. These qualities still existed. He passed his hands over the figure wonderingly, caressing it. He was lost in reverie; Mrs. Kasser, glowing with the success of her gift, turned to go. He looked up.

"Thank you, I've missed art," he said.

Oblivious of the war raging above them in the streets, the two sat for a few minutes talking about things that recalled life outside the inferno. The Kassers had long been art collectors. Wallenberg had not yet had the opportunity to start a collection, but as an architect he had a special feeling for three-dimensional structure. He loved sculpture. Now he had an important item for the start of a collection.

Before she left, Mrs. Kasser reminded him that she expected him for a Christmas Day luncheon tomorrow.

Christmas luncheon? Mrs. Kasser was an incorrigible optimist. How many of the invited guests would be alive tomorrow?

Mrs. Kasser was, in fact, a realist. She recognized that if they remained alive they would have to continue the struggle, and at that moment they all desperately needed a life-affirming pause. A few days before Christmas she had gone to the family farm to pick up her children—Michael, four, and Mary, two. She had sent them there with their governess to be away from the bombings in the city while she and her husband continued the Red Cross work. But then she feared to leave them away from her when the Russians came in. She had come back from the country with the children, as well as a cow and calf in back of a truck. She had put the cow in the garage to insure milk for the children and had the calf slaughtered and cooked for the luncheon. She had managed to get a Christmas tree and small gifts for her guests, Swedish diplomats and Red Cross officials.

There was real reason for rejoicing at the luncheon. First, for Budapest, the end of the war seemed near. The Russians seemed to have closed the ring around the capital during the night. Second, nearly all of the invited guests showed up, although several of them had escaped a close call at the hands of the Arrow Cross the day before.

The problem had started a few days earlier when Acting Foreign Minister Ladislaz Vöcsköndy had warned the Swedes that it was time to pack up and leave Budapest. The Hungarian government had retreated to Sopron, Western Hungary. Wallenberg, of course, would not leave the Budapest Jews to their fate at the hands of the Nazis. The legation had decided to remain—although the foreign office had said they were free to make their own decision about whether to remain or return to Stockholm. Furious, Vöczköndy reminded Anger that the Swedish Ministry of Foreign Affairs had refused to recognize the Arrow Cross government in October and at that time had given him only two hours to leave Stockholm.

On the morning of December 24, the legation building was

invaded by a troop of armed Arrow Crossmen, determined to take the entire staff off to Western Hungary. Two Swedish Red Cross workers living in the house next door to the legation, Margareta Bauer and Asta Nilsson, were carried off to the ghetto and their lives were threatened. Lars Berg and several staff members had been seized. Yet, through Red Cross official intervention, everyone had come through safely.

At the luncheon, they all felt full of hope. They talked about what they planned to do when the war was over. Wallenberg spoke about his rehabilitation plan. He said he would go back to Sweden and let the world know about the horrors of Budapest, and he was sure he would be able to raise the money for the necessary work of bringing families together, caring for the sick and restoring people to some semblance of normal life.

Wallenberg stayed on and talked with the Kassers after the others left. Again they spoke about art, about the end of the war. Wallenberg talked about how much he missed his family. He told about his mother and his sister, Nina, who had given birth to a daughter in the fall. He looked forward to seeing his first niece. He talked to Michael and Mary and told them he hoped they would never again go through such times as they were now experiencing.

It was a respite that must have strengthened him for the ordeals ahead. These were certainly the last happy hours he spent in freedom. When he got back to his office that day, he found out what had happened during the gentle interlude he had enjoyed. The following report was given by Maurice Lederer, director of the Orphans' Home at 5-7 Munkácsi Mihály Street, after the war:

On December 24th, eve of Christendom's love feast, the Nazis put in an appearance once more, rounded up all creatures alive including even the typhus-sick children, recognized as such by the medical officer, and those having fever as well, and led them over the Chain Bridge to Radetsky Barracks, from where owing to diplomatic intervention, the column of children was turned back to Pest. This was because the manager had gotten away and informed the right sources. But the conducting Nazi misunderstood the order given him to lead the group to Síp Street and led part of it to an evacuated Jewish house in Sziv Street and the other part to another house of Sziv Street.*

---

*YIVO Institute for Jewish Research, Archives on Holocaust in Hungary, Vol. III, p. 333.

(The "diplomatic intervention" Lederer referred to may have been Wallenberg's, but this is not certain. Anger recalls that late that night Wallenberg turned up at his [Anger's] Uri Street hideout apartment and that they spent the night behind barricaded doors with pistols nearby.)

But the trouble at the children's shelter did not end on Christmas Eve. On Christmas Day, the Nazi janitor of the building evidently called the *Nyilas* officials and told them that children were "escaping." The report continues:

The children—the smallest of whom were two to three years of age— were already the second day without the least food, in spite of the manager sending there the kitchen. The Nazi-minded janitor prevented the food from reaching the children who awaited, starving and freezing, what was to happen to them. At 4 P.M., the janitor appeared with an armed Nazi, who lined the children up, pretending, so the janitor said, that some of the children had escaped. After counting them twice he had to admit this was not true, and he left, but not without hitting the wife of the manager on the head with a hand grenade, which however, did not explode and caused only trifling bodily harm.

After about 5 P.M., five or six Nazis, following a denouncement by the janitor, stormed the building, broke the door like thunder and ordered that everybody line up in the court, leaving behind all their belongings, as these they would have no use for anyway. The panic among the starving, freezing, sick, feverish children passes description; the manager and the teaching staff hardly were able to restore order. We had to stay in the court for more than an hour at a temperature of eight to ten degrees Celsius below zero until the leading Nazi finished counting the crowd. Alas! A boy and a girl, 14 to 15 years old were shot dead on the spot.

After these shocks we left Sziv Street and marched through Teréz Boulevard and Váci Boulevard, the children weeping aloud. Although an immense number of people witnessed this march, doleful beyond imagination, not one of them uttered a word in our favor, though at that time, Pest being already surrounded by the Russians, this would perhaps have been helpful to us.

At Gomb Street the column halted, and the Nazis held counsel into which part of the Danube we ought to be thrown. Meanwhile an immensely strong Russian air raid occurred and it was as if they were just over our heads. The Nazis, fearing their lives, shouted: "Now run where you can!" whereupon the manager with 50 to 60 children, supposing in the dark that the others were following their example, ran into a side street. One part of the children thus got outside of shooting range of the Nazis, others ran to the residence of the International Red Cross in Munkácsi Mihály Street and others sought shelter in houses nearby. All this went on whilst the Nazis were firing after the runners. In one house the Nazis shot three children out of four whom the janitor had given up; this was in Petnehazy Street, whilst in another place three more children and Joseph Csillag, an excellent teacher, who had served in our asylum 31 years, were killed. The rest reached the institute in the course of the night.

The wife of the manager was wounded, yet could drag herself to the Red Cross building during the night. She found there already 40 to 50 children, who had been rescued from the very grip of death.

Director Lederer did not explain in his report that it was his wife who was wounded.

A meeting at the Swedish Embassy the following day brought out additional details. While the house at Munkácsi Mihály Street was being raided, another band of Arrow Cross soldiers and civilians entered a shelter at Vilma Kiralyno Street 25. There two old women between 70 and 80, two three-year-olds in the sickroom and a one-and-a-half-year-old were shot. A nurse who wanted to bundle up the sick children was shot. The others in the shelter were taken on a march to Radetzky Barracks and on the way a lame 13-year-old boy who could not keep up with the others was shot. A 14-year-old boy who had been shot in the leg and was therefore unable to go down to the courtyard was shot dead in the house.

From Christmas Eve on, the Arrow Cross attacks became more frequent and more violent. There had been a preholiday order by Ernö Vajna, the minister for the defense of Budapest, that all Jews in hiding must report to the Jewish Council at Síp Street for "relocation." The Arrow Cross gangs did their utmost to flush them out. They were largely unsuccessful in getting out the thousands, including children, from convents, monasteries and other church institutions, although they tried repeatedly. Many among the thousands who bribed Christians to hide them were betrayed and turned in. On the other hand, many Christians who helped Jews were accorded the same treatment as Jews. Even

Christians who did not commit the crime of helping Jews were in danger because the gangs made split-second street decisions.

Frustrated in their efforts to get as many of the hidden Jews as they had hoped, the terrorist gangs headed for the hospitals. On December 28 the Jewish Hospital on Bethlen Square was attacked by a mixed gang of Arrow Crossmen and SS. Patients were pulled out of beds and the personnel terrorized for twenty-four hours until a group of twenty-eight young men were taken away to a building on Wesseleyni Street, where they were murdered two days later.

Robbery became an important incentive in the killing spree. Jews pulled out of buildings were first stripped and robbed, then often killed in the street or dragged to the banks of the Danube for killing games. The corpses found in the street revealed that the victims had been mercilessly tortured. The more fortunate were simply shot and thrown into the river.

Some survivors, wounds stanched by the icy-cold water, managed to swim to shore, clamber out of the river and make their way to a hospital or protected house. When the Danube froze over there were more killings in the streets.

New Year's Eve was celebrated by the Arrow Cross with an attack on the "Glass House" at 29 Vadász Street. Some twenty-five hundred Jews under Swiss protection had been crowded in there, including many of the Zionist youth who were forging papers and deserters from labor service companies. When forty to fifty Arrow Crossmen stormed in firing and throwing hand grenades on New Year's Eve, one of their first victims was the mother of Rabbi Alexander Scheiber, an eminent scholar of Hungarian-Jewish culture and today head of the Jewish Theological Institute, the only Jewish seminary remaining in East Europe. The rabbi and his brother, Dr. Leopold Scheiber, today a prominent surgeon in New York, carried their mother to a makeshift hospital where a doctor attempted, unsuccessfully, to operate by candlelight.

The result of that raid was unsatisfactory from the Arrow Cross point of view. Only two beside Mrs. Scheiber were killed and twenty wounded. The gang turned eight hundred out into the street for "relocation," but Arthur Weisz, the former owner of the building, attempted to "negotiate" with the gang leaders. He eventually managed to get help from Pál Szalai, the Arrow Cross member who had also helped Wallenberg in emergency situations. The Budapest police intervened in the situation, and the eight hundred were returned to the house.

The following day Weisz was lured into a trap with an invitation from the Arrow Cross for further "negotiations." He left the house and was never seen again. On the same day Ottó Komoly, the Zionist member of the Jewish Council, was pulled out of his hiding place, the Ritz Hotel, and killed. Five days later another member of the Jewish Council, Miklós Szegö, was picked up on the street and killed. János Gábor, a third member of the council, had been killed by a gang weeks earlier.

During this period, Wallenberg's work was a minute-to-minute operation, conducted on several different levels:

First, he kept the lines of communication open with informers, seeking weak links in the Nazi chain. Late one night early in January he came to the legation building with a "Mr. Szabó." Wallenberg identified the man as a very high level Arrow Cross contact who promised to keep him notified about any developments in the plot to blow up the ghetto. Szabó also assigned guards to Wallenberg and the legation.

Second, he kept up his fight on the diplomatic level, preserving the fiction that he was dealing on a rational level with a sane government. The Arrow Cross government issued purely sadistic ordinances in the days before the Russians entered the city. It called for the removal of the thirty-five thousand Jews in the international ghetto to the starving, seriously overcrowded large ghetto. This, according to Arrow Cross threats, was preliminary to extermination of the entire ghetto by machine-gun fire.

Wallenberg, at this point assuming full authority for the Swedish legation, addressed an appeal and detailed memorandum to the German commander. He cited conditions in both ghettos. He noted that the large ghetto holding fifty-three thousand was unheated, that most people had no mattresses and many more had no blankets, that the tenements were being used as hospitals, that there was no soap and little water and that the daily allotment of food per person was nine hundred calories, as compared with thirty-six hundred for a soldier and fifteen hundred for prisoners. He noted that supplies of salt, vegetables and flour, which had been promised, had never been delivered, and that the Red Cross had intervened to fill the gap, but that these supplies were running low. He predicted famine within two days.

Wallenberg also pointed out the fifty-three thousand were already living in an area originally inhabited by fifteen thousand.

"For humane reasons this plan must be described as utterly crazy and inhuman," declared the memorandum. "The Royal Swedish Legation is not aware of any similar plan ever having been carried out by any other civilized government."

He appealed to have the order remanded.

The appeal failed. On January 4, four of the Swedish houses were evacuated; the inhabitants were first stripped of everything they owned, including their ration cards. The evacuation of the other Swedish houses was to be continued the following day, but Wallenberg managed to secure a delay of twenty-four hours and then of another forty-eight hours. This was revoked when it was reported that a patrol had been shot at from one of the Swedish houses.

In view of the prevailing barbarism, Wallenberg's polite diplomatic communications and his references to a "breach of extraterritoriality"—that is, the invasion of places ostensibly belonging to Sweden—appear absurd. Yet it was through the fiction that some semblance of civilized order existed that he was able to perform a few more lifesaving acts.

The most important was making a deal with Budapest Defense Minister Ernö Vajna to turn over some of the Swedish legation's food stocks in exchange for protection from *Nyilas* gangs. At this point hunger in the city was so serious that when a horse died in the street, a swarm of people carrying knives and other implements immediately attacked the carcass. People were exchanging valuable jewelry for bits of bread. Wallenberg's foresight in stocking as much food as possible in the fall turned out to be an important factor in the rescue operation. In offering some of his food stocks he asked that Vajna "restrain hotheads among the party members."

It is possible that Vajna tried or actually succeeded in carrying out his part of the bargain on one or more occasions, but on January 8 a gang invaded several "protected" houses, including a Swedish house at 1 Jókai Street. More than 300 "protected" Jews were brought to Arrow Cross headquarters at 14 Varoshaz Street, where they were tortured by Father András Kun and his accomplices. Later nearly 160 men were executed near the Danube.

It was shortly after this that Elizabeth Kasser saw Wallenberg for the last time. She had sought him out to tell him that the Arrow Cross had captured her husband. She, the children and their governess escaped and she had taken the children to a new refuge. When she reached Wallenberg at his office in the cellar in one of the buildings on Üllöi Road, she found him pale and shaken, more agitated than she had ever seen him. He told her what had happened on Jókai Street. He also said that he had just heard on the radio that a search was out for him and her husband. He correctly deduced that her husband had already managed to escape.

At this point he took cover in the house at Benzcur Street. Stephen Rádi recalls Wallenberg's saying, "They are looking for me." He was pale, unshaven and haggard. Nevertheless, he went on nightly excursions along with the Red Cross group in the house to bring bread to the ghetto, and he turned up at intervals at one or another of his offices.

Shortly before the Russians entered the city, photographer Tom Veres rushed to him, panic in his eyes.

"They've taken my parents!" he cried. His parents had been living in a building on Väröszmarty Square, and an Arrow Cross band, marauding for food, found them there along with a Swiss family. The Swiss had managed to get free, but not Tom's parents.

"Too late, Tom," Wallenberg had to say, looking into the young man's anguished face. "I can do nothing any more."

They shot Tom's parents into the Danube.

Wallenberg returned to the house on Benczur Street and waited for the Russians.

TEN

MESSAGES FROM MOSCOW

At the time Raoul Wallenberg stepped into his car in Pest, ostensibly to set out for Debrecen with his Russian escorts, his Swedish colleagues were going through an ordeal of their own.

When the Russians entered Pest, the Germans retreated over the Danube into Buda, blowing up all the bridges behind them. The Russians were already in sections of Buda, fighting from street to street. The troops in Pest kept up a rain of shellfire from their side of the Danube.

For a full month Buda was daily bombed from the air, battered by artillery fire and raked by machine-gun fire from low-flying fighter planes. The Swedish Embassy staff, like all the civilians, hid in cellars and existed as they could without gas, electricity or the normal water supply. People washed with melted snow and boiled snow over fires to make tea or soup.

In his book *With Raoul Wallenberg in Budapest,* Per Anger

relates that during an air raid a horse belonging to a German unit got shot near the door of his house:

We were not slow to join the swarm of people who hurried from all directions, brandishing knives and other instruments, to get themselves a piece of horse meat. It was a macabre sight. Old and young, women in furs and poor laborers, all crowded eagerly around the cadaver of the horse, attempting to chop the largest piece they could. In a short while, nothing was left of it but bones. We lived for several days on Hungarian horse goulash, skillfully prepared by the baroness. [The baroness owned the building in which Anger lived.]

By the end of January the first Russian soldiers entered the Swedish legation building. The Swedes were surprised to find themselves treated with something less than diplomatic politeness. They were required to turn over watches and other valuables. The Russians decided to take over the building for the billeting of soldiers. At this point Minister Danielsson was hiding in a cave with the Turkish ambassador, who had suffered a broken back as the result of one of the bombings, and the Papal Nuncio. When the Swedish minister later confronted Russian officers, he strongly protested the violation of the "extraterritorial rights of a neutral," particularly of a nation that protected the rights of thousands of Russian prisoners of war deposited by the Germans in Hungary after their battles on the eastern front. According to Anger, Danielsson was told that "the representatives of a country which through its iron ore deliveries to Germany had helped prolong the war, ought to keep his mouth shut."

The Russians pointed out, further, that the Swedes had no Russian-language documents to prove that they represented the Soviet Union in Budapest. (It is customary for neutral legations to assume the interests of belligerent powers during wartime.) Both Anger and attaché Lars Berg, who was directly responsible for looking out for Soviet interests, believe that things might have gone better for them and for Wallenberg if their home office had supplied them with the proper Russian-language documents. The foreign office has not explained this failure. It may have been simple negligence. But the official Russian-language documents might have prevented the takeover of the legation building by the Russian military.

The Russians proceeded to loot the building and blow up its

safe, which contained not only diplomatic papers but a large cache of securities and jewelry brought there for safekeeping by Swedish citizens and Hungarian Jews under Swedish protection. A large wooden box containing Wallenberg's papers was seized.

Unknown to the others, attaché Berg had been picked up in Pest by the NKVD and questioned for many hours about what the Swedes were up to in Budapest. He was questioned about Wallenberg's capitalist family, about where all the money in the Swedish Embassy coffers came from and where Wallenberg's money came from. Further, he was asked who was the head of espionage in the legation—he or Wallenberg. Berg denied any association of the Swedes with espionage and explained Wallenberg's rescue mission to the best of his ability. He was finally released. Hundreds of others connected with the Swedish, Swiss, Vatican and Red Cross staffs were questioned and released. Others were kept in prison for months, subjected to interrogations again and again.

Among those imprisoned by the Russians for months in Hungary was George Wilhelm, organizer of the Red Cross house on Benzcur Street. In 1980, living in retirement in Brussels, Wilhelm recalled being questioned mainly about Red Cross activities. The Swiss consul, Harald Feller, was brought to Moscow and imprisoned there for a year. The Swiss got him back through an exchange in which they turned over to the Russians six spies they had captured in Switzerland. The Russians were obviously suspicious of all outsiders in Budapest.

The war raged on in Buda until February 14. It ended when the Germans tried to break out through what they perceived as a weak spot in the vise around the city. It was a trap. The Russians waited until the last column of Germans marched into the open, and then annihilated the garrison to a man. They left behind ten thousand wounded in a makeshift hospital.

During most of the fighting the Swedish diplomats were held by the Russians in the countryside south of Budapest, where they were reasonably well treated. When the fighting ended they were brought back to Budapest. Buda lay in ruins, with fifty thousand civilian bodies buried beneath the rubble. The legation building had been completely pillaged by Russian soldiers.

The Swedes were held in the city until the Russians got orders about what to do with them. Nobody knew where Wallenberg was, but his colleagues hoped and assumed that he had reached Debrecen and left from there for Stockholm. On March 20 the entire Swedish staff, except for Wallenberg, was loaded on a bus and taken to Bucharest.

In March the Swedish Foreign Office, known as the UD, learned that there had been a broadcast over Hungarian Kossuth Radio that Wallenberg, who had disappeared along with his driver on January 17, had probably been murdered by Gestapo agents. The UD put through a series of messages asking the Russians for an investigation. They did not receive any replies.

In the meantime the Swedish legation was slowly traveling home—from Bucharest by train through Odessa, Moscow, Leningrad, Helsinki to Åbo, Finland, and from there by ferry to Stockholm. In Moscow the group met Swedish Minister Söderblom. Anger relates that Söderblom "displayed evident nervousness at our arrival. Had he feared that the Russians, instead of allowing us to travel to Sweden, would shunt our train onto the tracks to Siberia?"

Anger goes on to say that Söderblom then took him aside and warned: "Remember, when you get home to Sweden—not one harsh word about the Russians!" Wallenberg was at that moment sitting in a jail cell in Moscow.

The group arrived home on April 17, nearly a month after they had set out from Budapest.

At a press conference an hour after their arrival, reporters learned about the struggles of the embassy against the Hungarian Arrow Cross. They spoke of Wallenberg's heroism on behalf of the Budapest Jews and the help given by the Swedish Red Cross. The newsmen had a great story and rushed back to their offices. Nothing was said about the Russians. The members of the legation obeyed their own minister's warning in Moscow.

On April 26, 1945, *The New York Times* carried a succinct article about a Raoul Wallenberg who had played a heroic role in the rescue of twenty thousand Budapest Jews. The article said that he had "disappeared" on January 17. It mentioned his granduncle Axel, the former Swedish minister to the United States; his granduncle K. A. Wallenberg, Sweden's foreign minister during World War I; and his aunt, Mrs. William M. Calvin of Greenwich, Connecticut, married to Colonel William M. Calvin, a former American military attaché serving in the Scandinavian countries in both world wars. It gave some details about the rescue operation, but did not mention the War Refugee Board. The story of Raoul Wallenberg was of minor importance for a world in the final convulsions of World War II.

Sweden emerged from the war passionately committed to good relations with her powerful Soviet neighbor to the east. The foreign office felt satisfied with Sweden's success in keeping out of the war, even though it meant bending to German might. Now the government had no desire to tangle with the force that threw back the great German war machine at Stalingrad and was sweeping through East Europe like an avalanche.

Söderblom's warning to Anger that there was to be "not one harsh word about the Russians!" was in line with Swedish policy. Soviet Ambassador Mme. Kollontay's advice to make no "fuss" about Wallenberg was taken very seriously.

By early April Sweden was no doubt aware that a chill was setting in in the relationship between the West and the Soviet Union. Sweden planned to preserve her traditional neutrality, with a healthy regard for her physical security. She stood at the doorstep to the Soviet Union. Thus, on April 10, when U.S. Ambassador to Moscow Averell Harriman, at the instructions of the U.S. State Department, offered American help to Sweden in making inquiries on the Wallenberg case, Söderblom somewhat curtly declined the offer, stating the Swedes would manage on their own and that the Russians were making every possible effort on the case.

The fact that Söderblom was more concerned with pleasing the Russians than with finding Wallenberg is indicated in his exchange with the foreign office in July of 1945. The UD reported that there was a rumor in Switzerland that Wallenberg was living incognito in Budapest. Söderblom cabled back that he would now withhold a new query on the case because Wallenberg might turn up somewhere and "tell sensational stories to the press" about the Russians. His office cabled back to tell him to pursue the question—the story was only a rumor. Söderblom replied that in that case, it would not be appropriate to continue the queries.

It should be recalled that Söderblom was the diplomat who kept silent about the horrendous communication given to him by Baron von Otter in August 1942—Kurt Gerstein's eyewitness report that the

Nazis had "corpse factories" in East Europe and were killing masses of people with a new gas.

Nevertheless, prodded by the UD and the Swedish public, Söderblom made a half dozen more approaches to the Soviet about Wallenberg in 1945 and 1946. In June 1946, before leaving Moscow for a new assignment, Söderblom requested an interview with Stalin. Stalin normally did not receive ambassadors, except those from the United States and Great Britain. Söderblom was appreciative of the favor shown him and sent his office a positive account of Stalin's friendliness and appearance. He described Stalin as having "a short but well-proportioned body and regular features." Toward the end of the interview he discussed the Wallenberg case and told the Russian dictator that he personally believed that Wallenberg had been killed in an accident or by bandits, but that his government would appreciate further investigation. Stalin listened to the details, wrote down Wallenberg's name on a slip of paper and promised to look into the matter.

The details of this interview were not made known to the public until January 1980, when the UD opened a new White Book concerning the case. It created a furor in the Swedish press. From the vantage point of 1980, it seemed clear that Söderblom had not only indicated that Sweden wished to avoid "a fuss" about the Wallenberg matter; he had closed the door to further approaches. Once an appeal had been made to Stalin personally, lower-level officials would be unwilling to get involved in the issue. His statement that he believed Wallenberg had been been killed outside of Budapest offered Stalin an easy out. Tage Erlander, who was Sweden's Social Democratic prime minister between 1946 and 1969, thought the conversation between Stalin and Söderblom was "dangerous and perhaps disastrous." Erlander thought, "It would have been better if it had never taken place."

Söderblom, speaking up from retirement, defended himself in the Swedish press by stating that he had done his best by going to the highest authority in Russia. He said he had to show Stalin that he was not accusing the Russians of doing away with Wallenberg. He added that he had declined American help because it might have intensified Russian suspicions that Wallenberg was a spy.

In 1946 Söderblom's argument may have seemed reasonable, but in 1980 it appeared to be a poor rationalization for an overly timid approach to the issue. Söderblom's successor, a chargé d'affaires, Ulf Barck-Holst, took a more aggressive approach. He noted that whenever he raised the issue of Wallenberg the Russians brought up the matter of some people they wanted from Sweden. One was the daughter of a high Red Army officer who had defected to Sweden and the others were political refugees from the Baltic states. Barck-Holst suggested to his Foreign Office that an offer of an exchange be made. However, Swedish policy would not permit exchanging people who had found asylum. The matter was not pursued.

The case could have been pursued more forcefully if Sweden had confronted the Soviet with some evidence that Wallenberg was, in fact, in the Soviet Union. The Foreign Office actually had some evidence, but failed to use it. Edward af Sandeberg, a Swedish journalist who had been arrested in Berlin, was released from prison in June 1946. He told the Foreign Office that in the Soviet Union he had encountered two prisoners, one a Rumanian and the other a German, who told him that they had heard about a Swedish diplomat named Wallenberg in prison. Östen Undén, the Swedish Foreign Minister, considered af Sandeberg a Nazi and for that reason disregarded his report. Nine years later the German prisoner, Erhard Hille (see appendix), came out of Russia and verified Sandeberg's report. Hille had shared a cell with Langfelder in Lefortovo Prison and heard about Wallenberg through him.

Maj and Fredrik von Dardel did not give up. Their cause was joined by Rudolph Philipp, an Austrian Jewish journalist who had settled in Sweden. He had a strong background in Central European affairs and became convinced that the Russians were holding Wallenberg. He presented his reasons for believing Wallenberg was alive in a Russian jail in a book, *Raoul Wallenberg*, published in Stockholm in 1946. In it he scathingly attacked the Swedish government for negligence.

The UD renewed its queries to the Russians. On August 18, 1947, two years and eight months after Wallenberg vanished, Deputy Foreign Minister Andrei Vishinsky responded that Wallenberg was not known in the Soviet Union and had probably been killed by the Nazis during the fighting in and around Budapest. It was the first official response made to Swedish inquiries.

By this time Swedish public opinion had become aroused. A Swedish citizen, Mrs. Birgitta de Wylder-Bellander, became the moving force in a group known as the Wallenberg Action. Ingrid Gärde-Widemar, Swedish Supreme Court justice, developed a special interest in the case and gave her support to the group.

In 1948 Wallenberg's old colleague Per Anger was called home from Cairo to serve in the UD's political department in Stockholm. He was placed in charge of the case. He had always believed that Wallenberg had been taken prisoner by the Russians; the evidence that had reached the foreign office in the last three years reinforced his belief. However, he experienced total frustration in dealing with the case. He felt that Foreign Minister Östen Undén's attitude was simply negative.

In a confrontation with Undén, he called the minister's attention to the fact that the Swiss, the Italians and the Danes had all gotten back diplomats who had been taken prisoner by the simple expedient of making an exchange for Russians wanted by the Soviet. He also noted that Sweden had given Russia a billion crowns in credits during the 1946 trade negotiations and returned Russian spies without asking anything in return. Undén's reply was, "The Swedish government does not do such things."

At another time a meeting was arranged between Undén and members of the Wallenberg Action group, and Undén asked Mrs. Bellander, "Do you think Vishinsky is lying?"

Mrs. Bellander said she did. Undén's response was, "This is terrible, this is terrible!"

Anger, caught between his role as an employee of the foreign department and his sympathy for the Wallenberg advocates, asked to be relieved of the case in 1951; he did not return to it until his retirement from the diplomatic service in 1980.

Undén's attitude was castigated by Carl-Fredrik Palmstierna, private secretary to King Gustav VI Adolph between 1951 and 1973. In his memoirs, *The Feather in My Hand*, he describes Undén as "a Marxist professor of law," and says he "followed with benevolent interest the great socialist experiment in Russia, and he allowed nothing to interfere with Sweden's friendly relations with the Soviets." He maintains that the king was loyal to the minister and would countenance no criticism of his handling of the case.

Palmstierna also describes his own efforts to enlist the aid of Dag Hammarskjöld when he became general secretary to the United Nations in 1956. Hammarskjöld responded that the fact that he himself was a Swede made it doubly "difficult for him to put the case of a compatriot to the Russians." Palmstierna reflects that "If Hammarskjöld had assumed the case of a non-Swedish citizen, he would probably have been snubbed with the answer that, as secretary general to the United Nations, he had no right to meddle with internal questions in other countries." Palmstierna attributes Hammarskjöld's attitude to "that damned foreign office spirit! Of course there was no question of 'declaring war on Russia for the sake of Wallenberg,' as he [Hammarskjöld] repeated on a later occasion, quoting Undén."

In 1949, in response to an appeal by Wallenberg's brother, Guy von Dardel, Secretary of State Dean Acheson again offered American help to the Swedish government in making new approaches to the Soviet. Again the United States was turned down, this time by the Swedish representative in Moscow, Rolf Sohlman, who said "We cannot drive tandem with the Americans."

The Wallenberg Action group persisted, and on March 10, 1956, a new Swedish note was presented to the Russians, containing fresh evidence from returned prisoners stating that they had been in contact with Wallenberg (see appendix). The note contained a statement signed by Supreme Court Justices Rudolf Elklund and Erik Lind that they were convinced of the truth of the evidence.

The Kremlin responded that the testimony of "war criminals" could not be accepted. The answer was the same—Wallenberg was not known in the Soviet Union.

A few weeks later Prime Minister Tage Erlander, on an official visit to Moscow, brought the Wallenberg case to the attention of new Communist party Chairman Nikita Khrushchev. He got the old reply. However, he also got a promise that the Russians would study the documents he had brought with him concerning the case and would look into the matter further.

In February 1957, nearly a year later, came a reply which stunned the Swedish Foreign Office. It was from Russian Deputy Foreign Minister Andrei Gromyko, who reported that a new thorough search of the prison archives had turned up a handwritten report dated July 17, 1947, from the medical chief of Lubianka, addressed to the Minister for Security Service Abakumov:

"I report that the prisoner Walenberg [sic] who is known to you, died suddenly in his cell last night, probably following a myocardial infarction [heart attack]."

At last the Russians admitted he had been a prisoner in Moscow!

The Swedish government never saw a copy of this document and was never presented with a death certificate. The Soviet government keeps meticulous records on prisoners, yet in this case Wallenberg's name was misspelled and no information given as to age or citizenship. The reported note was in the nature of a casual memorandum. When the foreign office asked for details, they were informed that the doctor who signed the note was dead; Security Minister Abakumov was dead, shot for "criminal activities"; and his chief, Beria, Stalin's notorious head of security and hatchet man, had also been shot for "criminal activities." The medical chief, A.L. Smoltsov, was also dead. Furthermore Smoltsov had written a note at the bottom of the report: "Have personally informed the minister. Order has been given of cremating of the corpse without post-mortem examination." The message now was that Wallenberg had been a victim of Stalinist excesses and the Soviet government expressed regrets to the Swedish government. From the Russian point of view the case was now closed.

Although many in Sweden would have been satisfied to accept the Soviet version of what happened to Wallenberg, those who had mistrusted the Soviet all along pointed out that the Russians' admission that they had done wrong for twelve years was no reason to believe them now. They had treated some twenty Swedish requests for a thorough investigation with disdain, sometimes not responding for years, and at other times responding with a curt "not known in the Soviet Union." Why should they be believed now? Why had the Soviet government failed to produce a proper death certificate? Why were there no details aside from the perfunctory supposedly long-lost memorandum? Physicians called attention to the fact that it would be unusual for a man of Wallenberg's age and good heredity to die of a heart attack.

Moreover, the Swedish Foreign Office had information which suggested the possibility that Wallenberg was in the prison at the city of Vladimir, about one hundred miles east of Moscow, in the early fifties. They had withheld this material which was still being studied.

The information was studied by Supreme Court Justices Ragner Gyllensward and Per Santesson who reported in 1960:

The statements contain a large amount of information, the correctness of which it has been possible to check and they support each other. In our opinion, according to Swedish law, the present report must be considered to make it probable—though it does not contain full evidence in this respect—that Wallenberg was alive at least in the beginning of the 1950's and at that time in prison in Vladimir.

The next important step in the case was taken in 1961 when Nanna Svartz, an eminent professor of medicine of Sweden's Karolinska Hospital, went to Moscow for a conference. She decided to discuss the

Wallenberg case with Russian colleague Professor A. L. Myashnikov, with whom she had shared many scientific interchanges in the past. Myashnikov replied that he knew about Wallenberg. He had been very ill and was in a mental hospital.

Professor Svartz asked to be taken to him and Myashnikov agreed. However, her visa had run out and she was not able to arrange for its extension. She had to leave the next day.

Nanna Svartz returned home and advised Prime Minister Tage Erlander of what had occurred. Erlander immediately wrote an urgent message to Stalin's successor, Communist party chief Nikita Khrushchev. He cited Wallenberg's reported ill health and asked to have a Swedish doctor go to Moscow to see him and to discuss with Soviet physicians his condition and his transportation home.

There was no immediate reply. Professor Svartz returned to Moscow the following month and asked Myashnikov if she could now go to visit Wallenberg in the hospital. He responded that she would have to get permission from the authorities—and added, "unless he is dead." She immediately tried to contact Deputy Foreign Minister Semyonov, but failed. She returned to Stockholm.

Still there was no response from the Kremlin.

Professor Svartz went to Moscow for another medical conference in May 1962. This time Myashnikov said the issue could only be taken up through diplomatic channels. Erlander pressed the issue through diplomatic channels—to no avail. In March of 1964 Soviet Foreign Minister Gromyko visited Stockholm, and Erlander proposed to him that Professors Svartz and Myashnikov be brought together and questioned.

This brought an answer from Myashnikov that he knew nothing about Wallenberg, had never heard his name, and that the whole thing must have been a misunderstanding because he and Professor Svartz had been talking in German.

The two professors were finally brought face to face in July 1965 in the presence of Swedish and Russian officials and interpreters. Both stuck to their stories. Four months after this meeting Myashnikov died and Svartz questioned whether it was of natural causes. He appeared to her to have been a healthy man in his early sixties. As for Svartz—hale and cogent at the age of 90—she attended an international symposium on the Wallenberg case in January 1981 and asserted that there could not have been a misunderstanding.

In time, all but the most dedicated got tired of the case. It was easier to believe Wallenberg was dead; some said too much fuss was made over him. The man had been foolish, overzealous, overpassionate; people like that are bound to get into trouble. Of course it was sad for the mother, but the poor woman had been unable to resign herself to her loss and had become obsessed with the idea that Raoul was alive in Russia. New information repeatedly surfaced. In 1953 she was shocked to learn that some espionage work might actually have gone on at the Swedish Legation. A man who spoke Russian and carried a false Norwegian passport under the alias "Henrik Thomsen" was employed in Lars Berg's section, where he did office work and had the opportunity to see information from Russian prisoners. He was arrested by the NKVD and brought to Russia. It was believed he had been executed as a German spy until he turned up in Stockholm in 1953. He told Mrs. von Dardel that he had sent information from Budapest to a German contact. Rudolph Philipp suggested that Thomsen could have given false information about Wallenberg to win his own freedom from the Russians. The Swedish Foreign Office notified the Soviet that Wallenberg had nothing to do with Thomsen.

Despite the discouragement, Maj von Dardel would not give up. In 1967 she contacted Simon Wiesenthal. Could the great Nazi hunter help find a man imprisoned in the Soviet Union? It was a new kind of challenge for Wiesenthal. He immediately became fascinated with the case. He decided the most important thing to do was to get publicity outside of Sweden, so that people with information would come forward. He made a point of talking about Raoul Wallenberg in his frequent interviews with journalists.

Mrs. von Dardel also contacted Alexander Solzhenitsyn, author of the monumental study of life in Russian prison camps, *The Gulag Archipelago,* when in 1974 he came out of the Soviet Union to receive his Nobel Prize in Stockholm. Solzhenitsyn came to see her. He said he had read the large packet of documents she had sent him and he was convinced her son was alive in Russia. He recommended two steps to her: (1) Put an end to Swedish quiet diplomacy. Get international interest in the case. (2) Enlist the Jews. They will recognize their obligation in the case. And they are the only ones who have been successful in getting people out of Russia.

Jewish help came strangely and unexpectedly from Israel. In November 1977 a Russian-born dentist, Dr. Anna Bilder, had received a phone call from her father in Moscow, Jan Kaplan. Kaplan had been serving a four-year jail sentence for an "economic crime." He had been released before the end of his term because he suffered from a heart condition. He told his daughter he was feeling fine. How could he be fine after two years in jail, asked his daughter.

"It's possible," he answered. "In 1975 I met a Swede who told me he had been in prison for thirty years, and he seemed in good health."

Dr. Bilder, grateful that her father was well and out of prison, and knowing nothing about Wallenberg, mentioned the conversation to relatives in Israel, but saw no significance in it.

A year later another Russian Jewish emigré, Abraham Kalinski, read in a Russian-language Israeli newspaper that Wiesenthal had called upon Sweden to boycott the 1980 Moscow Olympics if the Russians refused to tell the truth about Wallenberg. Kalinski knew the name Wallenberg. He had heard about him from a fellow cellmate in Verchme Uralsk in the early fifties. His cell mate, an author named David Vendrovsky, said he had formerly shared a cell with a onetime Latvian cabinet minister, Wilhelm Munters, and a Swede named Wallenberg. Vendrovsky pointed out the two of them taking exercise in the prison yard. Later Kalinski saw Wallenberg again at Vladimir prison in 1959.

Kalinski was permitted to send a monthly postcard to his sister in Israel. On one of these cards he wrote that there were few foreigners at the prison besides himself (he is Polish), and that one of them was a Swede "who saved Rumanian Jews during the war." Kalinski was released from jail later that year, and during the seventies joined his sister in Israel. He discovered that she had saved his postcards, so he was able to verify the time at which he had seen Wallenberg.

When Kalinski learned that Wallenberg was being sought, he contacted Simon Wiesenthal in Vienna and told him about his contact with Wallenberg. He said that his informant on Wallenberg's wartime activities had probably confused Hungary with Rumania.

Kalinski then learned through Russian friends in Israel about the message Anna Bilder had received from her father. He contacted her and, at his urging, she gave the information to the Swedish Embassy representative in Israel.

On the basis of the information from Bilder and Kalinski, the Swedish Foreign Office sent the Russians a new query in January of 1979. They received the same answer, that their information was false and that there could be no news on the case.

Six months later Anna Bilder received a letter from her mother stating that her father had been taken back into custody, thrown into Lubianka prison and later taken to Lefortovo. Mrs. Kaplan said that it had all come about because her husband had tried to get a letter out of Russia telling about "that Swede." Kaplan, who evidently had no experience in political intrigue, handed the letter to one of the Soviet agents who routinely blend with the crowd of dissidents milling around the Moscow synagogue on the Sabbath.

Mrs. Kaplan later wrote to her daughter that she had been withholding the tragic news that her father had disappeared, she did not know to where. Dr. Bilder informed the Swedish Embassy. At this point Swedish Prime Minister Ola Ullsten contacted Alexei Kosygin and asked for a reopening of the case and the opportunity to speak to Kaplan. The same answer came back: Wallenberg had died in 1947. The request to interview Kaplan was ignored. He has not been heard from since February 1979.

Frustrated in her efforts to move the Swedish government, Maj von Dardel had long hoped to enlist American aid. In May 1973 she wrote to Secretary of State Henry Kissinger, seeking his intervention. She received a reply from Thomas R. Pickering, executive secretary, that a report and recommendation were being prepared for Kissinger. The report was presented with a recommendation that an inquiry on the case be made to the Soviet government, but Kissinger never okayed the query. The Swedes speculated that he was annoyed with Sweden because of her antagonistic position on the United States role in Vietnam. Lena Biörk-Kaplan, who headed the eastern section of the American Free Wallenberg Committee, said that Kissinger told her he had never seen the memorandum, that it must have been disposed of by a subordinate. He has twice responded with "no comment" to this writer's inquiries.

Two fundamental questions inevitably arise: First, why would the Russians keep Wallenberg alive for so many years? Second, why if he was still alive in 1957, wasn't he released at that time in view of the fact that the Russians were then willing to acknowledge that he had been a victim of Stalinist excesses?

A possible answer to the first question is that, apart from the Stalin era, execution has not been the Russian custom. Imprisonment, exile, labor camps and mental hospitals usually effectively take the place of actual killing. It is believed that Wallenberg might have been sentenced by the *Ossobenoye Soveschanive*, three-person committees set up in various areas to rule on politically suspicious prisoners in Stalin's time. The committees could make decisions without any trial. If Wallenberg had been sentenced to life imprisonment he could not have been killed deliberately except by a high-level order, and it is unlikely that those at the highest levels would violate custom and expose themselves to criticism by eliminating a person who, in Russian eyes, had already been rendered a non-person. (See final segment of the appendix to learn how prison authorities attempted to prevent the spread of information about Wallenberg and Langfelder.)

The answer to the second question is more complex. Wallenberg may have been in extremely poor mental and physical condition in 1957. It would have been too embarrassing to the Russians to return him at that time. The report from Nanna Svartz's colleague, Myashnikov, that Wallenberg was in poor condition in a mental hospital in 1961 would seem to substantiate this. However, Kalinski maintains that he saw Wallenberg for a second time in Vladimir prison in 1959, and Jan Kaplan's report specifically referred to the Swede's good health in 1975. Obviously, one or more of the reports could be in error. However, it is also possible that Wallenberg was mentally and/or physically ill at various periods and subsequently recovered, or that he was subjected for a time to "psychiatric treatment" with disorienting and debilitating drugs, a common Soviet way of handling political prisoners, as well-substantiated reports show.

Throughout the years many reports of sightings and hearsay accounts of sightings of a long-term Swedish prisoner or a Swede held in isolation have come through the Swedish Foreign Office. They are carefully screened and many are eliminated. Others are placed on file for further study. Sometimes long-buried scraps of information take on relevance as more substantive reports come in. Guy von Dardel, despite an active professional life as a nuclear physicist, vigorously pursued on his own every possible lead in the search for his brother.

Maj von Dardel and her husband Fredrik died within two days of one another in February 1979 at ages 86 and 93. They never gave up hope for Raoul and knew that their children Guy and Mrs. Nina Lagergren would carry on the struggle.

ELEVEN

THE MAN WHO WILL NOT DISAPPEAR

One of the most bizarre aspects of the Wallenberg case is the fact that for thirty-five years it remained shrouded in dense fog, virtually unknown outside of Sweden.

The recurring furors over the case in the Swedish press caused barely a ripple in the rest of the Western world. The Hungarian and Swedish books written about Raoul Wallenberg were never translated. Small Jewish-interest publications revived the story from time to time, usually ending with the statement that Wallenberg had "vanished" with the Russian soldiers and there was some mystery surrounding his fate. In April 1968 *True* magazine published an article presenting all the details that had come out about Wallenberg's imprisonment in the Soviet Union up to that date. The piece was written by Arthur D. Morse, author of *While Six Million Died*, a ground-breaking study pointing out the complicity of the free world in the Holocaust by showing repeated failures to react to Nazi atrocities. In his book, Morse cited Wallenberg as a shining exception to the prevailing apathy. However, in spite of the fact that Morse was the author of a highly regarded book and wrote a carefully documented article, he was unable to get it printed in a mainstream publication. *True* was an offbeat men's magazine emphasizing adventure and heroism. The same magazine printed an article about Wallenberg's exploits in Budapest in July 1947. Ralph Wallace was the author.

The reasons for the strange muffling of a story that could be expected to capture the public imagination lie buried in the pathology of postwar history. One element in that pathology was the reluctance of the world to talk about the Holocaust. The initial shock produced by the grisly discoveries in the death camps was followed by stunned silence. The survivors seemed to have lost their voices and the world preferred to forget them. The silence was broken from time to time by isolated scholarly books, the philosophical writing of Elie Wiesel, the popular play *The Diary of Anne Frank* based on a first-hand account, and the sensationalism surrounding the Eichmann trial in Israel. However, the world's failure to assimilate the facts about the Holocaust was proven when a pitifully inadequate and prettified TV mini-series based on the Holocaust produced amazement in the United States and Europe in 1979. The postwar world had failed to come to terms with facts of history that demanded a radical change in modern assumptions about human nature and social progress. In such a climate there could be no receptivity to the story of a man who had gone against the great tide of indifference to the Holocaust even while it was happening.

A second factor that interfered with exposure of the Wallenberg story was the widespread reluctance of respectable writers and politically influential individuals to question Soviet actions—a reluctance paradoxically bred in the Cold War atmosphere. Those who would normally respond to an important humanitarian issue did not want to be put in a position in which they could be accused of "Red-baiting" or contributing to Cold War propaganda. It became intellectually disreputable to call attention to large scale atrocities like the bloodbaths of the Stalin era on the ground that this might give the Soviet Union a bad image and help bring on World War III. Ambassador Söderblom's admonition, "Not one harsh word about the Russians," seemed to have echoed throughout the West. For example, when Prime Minister

Mackenzie King of Canada discovered in the year Söderblom issued his warning that the Soviet Embassy in Canada hosted a nest of spy masters commanding a small army of Canadian atom scientists and government aides, his main concern was how to cope with the situation without offending the Russians. He wrote in his diary (on file in the Canadian National Archives) that he feared a secret investigation of the Soviet's espionage activities "might cause Russia to feel that we had performed an unfriendly act."

It was not until the Russians themselves, through the writing of Solzhenitsyn and others and through the courageous efforts of the dissidents, revealed the post-Stalinist terrors in their own country that the taboo against criticism of Russia was lifted and a worldwide human rights movement sprang into being. Coincidentally, a new interest in the Holocaust developed as a new generation, which had been told little about it, began to ask questions.

In the new climate of opinion in the eighties it was possible for Wallenberg's story to become visible. The tragedy is that, like the Holocaust itself, visibility came too late.

The fact is that an appropriate concern about the fate of Wallenberg would not have offended the Russians to the point of declaring war, and it probably would not have seriously increased Cold War tensions. Over the years there were innumerable opportunities for the United States to bring up the Wallenberg case in the framework of talks about exchanges of prisoners or spies. Even if Wallenberg's mission had actually included some information work for the American or British government, it should have been possible to secure his release. Hundreds of out-and-out espionage agents have been exchanged during the time in which Wallenberg has been reported imprisoned. The Soviet government might have stuck by the story that he died in 1947, but with incentives, they also might have discovered another error. Who could know without trying?

The Wallenberg case finally emerged out of the fog into the clear view of the world through a gradual process.

It began with a small item in *The New York Times*, in November 1977, stating that Simon Wiesenthal had new information about a lost hero of World War II, Raoul Wallenberg, who was believed to be still alive in the Soviet Union. The story hit one American reader like a bolt of lightning. Her name was Annette Lantos. She and her husband Tom had been among the thousands who had lived through the Nazi reign of terror in Budapest. Like virtually all Budapest Jews, they believed that Wallenberg had been killed in 1945 by Nazis. They felt they owed their lives to him.

The Lantoses decided to look into the matter. They were in a good position to do so because Tom, a political economist, was at that time active in Washington as a senior policy advisor to U.S. Senators Joseph Biden and Frank Church, then chairman of the Senate Foreign Relations Committee. They quickly learned that there was ample reason to believe that Wallenberg was still alive.

Annette immediately thought of Wallenberg's mother in Stockholm and wrote to Maj von Dardel. She told her own story. When she was twelve years old her father was dragged out of a shelter by Hungarian Nazis, to be killed in the street. She and her mother were spared, and after the war they emigrated to Canada.

In 1950 Annette married a fellow Hungarian emigré, Tom Lantos. Tom had been an escapee from a forced labor camp at sixteen, and at seventeen became a student leader in the opposition to the Russian takeover in his country. He left Hungary for the United States in 1947. He won a scholarship to the University of Washington, and became an economics professor at the University of California, a pioneer in public and educational broadcasting and a well-known commentator on world affairs.

Annette raised two daughters. But in the midst of her happiness, she was haunted by the horrors of Budapest. She began to lecture to synagogue groups about the Holocaust. Again and again, she found herself talking about the power of one man to do good—Raoul Wallenberg. He had not only saved thousands of Jews, but had restored her belief in humankind.

Annette wanted to know how she and her husband could help in the search for Raoul Wallenberg. Mrs. von Dardel responded by inviting her to Stockholm. There, for the first time, thirty-two years after Wallenberg was captured, a Hungarian-American Jew learned all the agonizing details of the Wallenberg case. Annette returned home determined to do everything she could to fight for Wallenberg's life.

Annette and Tom Lantos launched a campaign to enlist the interest of American legislators, and to rouse American Jews and human-rights activists to the cause. Senators Frank Church (Democrat, Idaho), Claiborne Pell (Democrat, Rhode Island), Daniel Patrick

Moynihan (Democrat, New York) and Rudy Boschwitz (Republican, Minnesota) became cochairmen of a Free Wallenberg Committee. At the same time in England two members of Parliament, Greville Janner and Winston Churchill II, took up the case. American-Jewish organizations initiated programs to educate the public in the facts of the case.

In the fall of 1980 Tom Lantos was elected to Congress as representative from San Mateo County, California. He introduced the bill in the House of Representatives to make Raoul Wallenberg an honorary American citizen. The bill passed by 396 to 2. It was passed by the Senate unanimously.

My own involvement in the case began shortly after my return from Stockholm in 1979. At that time I noted a newspaper advertisement calling on Hungarian Jews and others to concern themselves with Wallenberg's fate. The advertisement had been signed by Annette and Tom Lantos. I contacted them and learned that they were trying to make Americans aware of the case. I told Mrs. Lantos that I had written many *New York Times Magazine* articles in the past, and I was sure the editors would be interested in this story.

The article appeared on March 30, 1980. Illustrated with some of the pictures taken by Tom Veres in Budapest and others showing Raoul as a child and youth in Stockholm, it created a storm of interest. It had a strong impact in Stockholm. The fact that the *Times* featured the article on the cover of its Sunday magazine put the case in a new perspective. Moreover, the story appeared just a few months after a new batch of White Papers had been released from the Swedish Foreign Office. These were the papers that had the Swedish press and TV in an uproar over what was almost universally regarded as the early bungling of the case, the failure to "put hard against hard" in dealing with the Russians.

The Wallenberg story was also shown on American and British television. Interviews with individuals whose lives had been saved by Wallenberg, as well as with Wallenberg's sister and brother and former colleagues in Budapest, brought the dramatic story into countless homes in the United States and Western Europe.

On January 15 and 16, 1981, the thirty-sixth anniversary of the seizure of Wallenberg by the Russians, a full review of the case and new reports that Wallenberg was still alive in 1980 were presented in

Stockholm before nearly one hundred representatives of the international press, radio and TV corps and human rights activists, as well as members of Free Wallenberg committees from all over the world.

It was a dramatic occasion, the first time so many people intimately concerned with the case had come together, and undoubtedly it was the last time, because the ages of the majority of participants ranged from the sixties through the nineties. Guy von Dardel, Nina Lagergren and Marcus Wallenberg represented the family; Per Anger and Lars Berg, Wallenberg's colleagues at the embassy, were also there. The Jewish concern in the case was reflected in the appearance of three world-renowned figures associated with the Holocaust and its aftermath—Simon Wiesenthal; Gideon Hausner, who was the Israeli government's chief prosecutor in Adolf Eichmann's trial in Jerusalem in 1961; and Elie Wiesel, philosophical chronicler of the Holocaust. Two prominent Swedes long dedicated to the Wallenberg cause, retired Swedish Supreme Court Justice Ingrid Gärde-Widemar and Professor Nanna Svartz, were available for interviews. Professor Svartz, hale and cogent at ninety-two, sat through the lengthy proceedings, ready to repeat for reporters who approached her individually her amazing experiences of 1961, when her colleague Professor Myashnikov told her that Wallenberg was in a mental institution and then later retracted the whole story.

The American interest in the case was represented by Annette Lantos; Elizabeth Moynihan, wife of Senator Patrick Moynihan; and Lena Biork Kaplan, a Swedish-American who heads the Free Wallenberg Committee of New York. Andre Lwoff, Nobel Prize winner in medicine, represented the Raoul Wallenberg Committee of France, and Greville Janner, M.P., represented a similar committee in Great Britain.

Wiesenthal released a story from a source he said he could only identify as I.L., who reported that he had been in close contact with Soviet war hero General G. Kuprianov, who had been imprisoned between 1948 and 1956. Kuprianov had kept notes, and he recorded that in 1953 he had encountered Raoul Wallenberg in a prison transport. (Released Soviet prisoners report that transports from one region to another occur frequently.) He met Wallenberg again in 1955 in a transport from Verschne Uralsk to Vladimir prison and for a third time in 1956 at the dentist's office in Vladimir prison. This information appeared in a Russian immigrant paper in New York, the *New Russian Word*, on January 1, 1979. Subsequently, Kuprianov was summoned by the KGB and questioned about his contacts with Wallenberg. At that time he learned to his surprise that Wallenberg had never been returned to Sweden. According to Kuprianov's information Wallenberg had been sentenced to twenty-five years in 1945 or 1946 and should have been released in 1970 or 1971.

In May of 1979 the article about Kuprianov's encounters with Wallenberg appeared in the Swedish daily *Svenska Dagbladet*, and Kuprianov was accused of collaboration with Western journalists. His interrogator said, "You who have been rehabilitated must help to refute these American-Israeli provocations," and Kuprianov replied, "We have already acknowledged the crimes of Beria, why cannot we then also acknowledge the crime against Wallenberg?" The KGB colonel replied, "We are not here to discuss the possible crimes of Beria, but the crimes of the American and Israeli intelligence agencies against the Soviet Union." Kuprianov was ordered to deny all the statements that he had met anyone named Wallenberg.

Kuprianov refused to issue a denial and was told that he would no doubt be ready to give in at his next questioning. He was called for a new questioning a few days later. Five days after he left, his wife was called and told to come to visit her husband in the hospital. When she arrived he was dead and in the morgue. She was told that the cause of death was "infarctus of the heart."

While Mrs. Kuprianov was at the hospital the KGB ransacked the apartment and removed all papers. She was ordered to tell any Western journalists who came to her home to ask for documents that she would have to look for the papers and take their names and addresses in order to get in touch with them later. In the meantime, she should inform the KGB.

Mrs. Kuprianov received such a visit, but the journalist got suspicious when she asked his name and address, and left. He did not show up again.

Journalists tried to get Wiesenthal to release more information about the indentity of I.L., but were unable to do so. Wiesenthal also reported that he had information from a generally reliable source that an "old Swede" in poor health was in 1978 in Blagoveshchensk Special Psychiatric Hospital in the Amur region, close to the Chinese border. He had been in confinement for a long time, perhaps since World War II. His name was unknown to the informants. His last report was of a Swede in a prison hospital in the Leningrad region in 1980. Many elderly foreign prisoners were kept there.

A highlight of the hearing was the presentation of two in-person witnesses. One, André Schimkevitch of Paris, had served twenty-eight years in Soviet prisons. He had been born in Russia of Russian parents. His parents had separated and his mother took him to Paris, where she remarried. When Schimkevitch was sixteen he traveled to Russia to visit his father. Soon after, he was imprisoned for espionage. He said that for two days in December 1947 he had shared a cell in Lubianka with the Swede Wallenberg. The time was five months after Wallenberg was supposed to have died.

How could Schimkevitch remember the date?

"One remembers everything in prison," he replied through tight lips.

Why had he not told his story before? He said he had in fact told it in 1958, after he was released. He had passed from Finland through Stockholm and made contact with individuals he believed to be members of the Wallenberg family. He had been invited to dinner in an elegant home, but he did not know the names or address of his host and hostess. The following day he left for Paris. His story had never been brought to the Swedish Foreign Office or to the von Dardels.

A strange story. Yet Elizabeth Kasser, who attended the hearings, was able to vouch for the fact that Schimkevitch had spent twenty-eight years in Russian prisons. She had known him in Paris—as the stepson of Jacques Lipchitz, the noted sculptor.

The second witness was Dr. Marvin Makinen, physicist of the University of Chicago, who had served three years of an eight-year sentence in Soviet prisons between 1961 and 1964. He had been an exchange student at the Free University of Berlin when he took a vacation trip to the Soviet Union. He was arrested for espionage in the city of Kiev and sentenced to two years in prison under a strict regime and the last six years in labor camp. He was in Vladimir prison at the same time as Francis Gary Powers, who had been picked up by the Russians after his U-2 spy plane had been downed, over the Central area of the Soviet Union.

Powers had been taking reconnaissance photos. Makinen was aware that Powers had as his cell mate a man named Zygurd Kruminsh, a Latvian. When Powers was released in February 1962, Makinen was transferred to Powers's former cell and inherited Kruminsh as cell mate. Makinen disliked and distrusted the man. His suspicions that Kruminsh was a KGB informer were reinforced when a fellow prisoner later said, "He got to sit with all the foreigners—with you, with Powers and with the Swede, van den Berg." Makinen wondered vaguely about the name—why would a Swede have a Dutch name?

I interviewed Makinen months after the hearing in New York. He added some interesting details. He said that after he was released from Russia in an exchange of prisoners in 1964 he had been debriefed by the State Department, and he spoke about Kruminsch and the Swede. He was asked to report that part of his story to the Swedish Embassy in Washington. He did. A year later he was invited to tell his story again to two representatives of the Swedish Embassy. When he finished he was asked not to talk to others about it.

It was not until March 1980, when he saw the article about Raoul Wallenberg in *The New York Times*, that Makinen suddenly realized that the correct name of the Swede must have been Wallenberg. (Non-English-speaking people pronounce the *W* as *V*—as the Swedes do.) Makinen noted in the article that Wallenberg's brother was Guy von Dardel, a scientist with whom he had some contact on professional matters. He immediately called him and gave him all the information he could about his stay in prison. Von Dardel said that the family had never been given the information Makinen reported to the Swedish Embassy.

Makinen said that although prison and labor camp were extremely difficult, he was aware that there were many long-term survivors. He had become very ill, and believed at times that he would never get out. However, he was sustained by an occasional visit from a representative of the American Embassy (he was supposed to receive a visit once in six months). "They would give you a list of things you couldn't talk about—one of them was food. But at least I knew the government was trying to get me out. And I knew my family was fighting for me." Makinen was finally released in an exchange along with the Reverend Walter J. Ciszek, S.J. (John XXIII Center for Christian Oriental Studies, Fordham University), who had spent more than twenty-five years in Soviet imprisonment.

Each story involving Wallenberg seems to raise more questions than can be answered. However, perhaps none is stranger than the fact that Raoul's cousins, Jacob and Marcus Wallenberg, were unable or unwilling to get involved in the case. I interviewed Marcus Wallenberg on that matter on the last afternoon of the hearings in a small, antiseptic-looking conference room of the head office of the Skandinaviska Enskilda Bank. It is a big slate-gray building and, true to the Wallenberg style of not being seen, it bears no sign on the outside.

I had been informed that Dr. Wallenberg had been greatly impressed with *The New York Times* article, partially because, on a visit to New York shortly after it appeared, a customs man had stopped him and asked him whether he was related to the Raoul Wallenberg who had saved the Jews of Budapest. He replied in the affirmative, and the man pumped his hand and with great emotion told him how honored he felt to meet a relative of so great a man. It may have been the first time a banking Wallenberg was congratulated on being related to Raoul.

Dr. Wallenberg—with startlingly large, brilliant blue eyes, tall, slender, pink-skinned—was extremely gracious and willing to talk about Raoul, but confessed that he had seen little of him because they had both been out of the country a great deal. He remembered Raoul's father as being "a very, very nice man" and a frequent visitor at his home before he became ill with cancer. He said he admired Raoul, Sr., for "his spirit, his initiative, his very amusing talk. He was very great fun."

I asked why the family didn't go around the foreign office to make their own contacts with the Russians. He replied: "Well, I can understand your question. You as an American are not used to dealing with a dictatorship, an extremely centralized and powerfully steered country. You see, at the time, it took a long time for people to realize what happened. And it was then in the hands of the government. To try to do anything in Russia, you know, outside the official channels, is absolutely bound to rebound. So what you had to do was to be careful all the time, to let it go. You talked, of course, to people in the government or in the bureaucracy. Raoul's mother, Mrs. von Dardel, was very active all the time. And the family was doing a lot, following it all with the greatest interest, all the time very mindful that they might hurt the case."

I pointed out that he had once been recommended as ambassador to Russia. He laughed and said that at one time Madame Kollontay had suggested it, but that was the last he had heard of it. I added that his companies had trade dealings with Russia—had he ever thought of calling up Stalin and asking him to look around for his cousin.

Dr. Wallenberg was vastly amused by the question. He replied, "I doubt very much whether that would have been the right thing to do."

"But what if you said to Stalin, 'You've made a mistake. My cousin was not a spy, but was on a humanitarian mission. And we would appreciate your releasing him. In return, we'd do something you'd like to have done.'"

"That would not have worked. We were as much engaged as anyone in the hope and the will, but we were very much advised not to do things which would be outside the diplomatic channels because it could hurt the case. And those who did things—you know, Professor

Svartz on her professional visits to Moscow—did raise these questions. But not the family."

My own later research in the Swedish Foreign Office documents on the case turned up an item Dr. Wallenberg may have forgotten. He sent a written appeal for help to Mme. Kollontay in Russia in 1946. She replied with a note in French, dated June 7, 1946. In it she thanked him for the gift he sent her, a painting of Prince Eugen. She said she would try to do something, but pointed out that as she was no longer in an official position there was no opportunity to "arranger les affaires" (loosely translated, work out deals). Her personal cordiality was evident in the note, as she said she had not forgotten the help Wallenberg gave her at a critical moment (presumably, the time he visited Finland to persuade the Finns to accept an armistice with the Soviet).

Swedish isolation on the case officially came to an end in the fall of 1980 when the United States and Sweden for the first time acted on the matter together. It was raised as a human rights issue in Madrid at the Conference on Security and Cooperation in Europe, a follow-up to the Helsinki Human Rights Accords. Max M. Kampelman, who headed the United States delegation to the conference, reported that he and the Swedish ambassador had worked in close cooperation.

At a semi-official Washington function following the signing of the bill making Wallenberg an honorary American citizen, a representative of the Swedish Embassy admitted with some emotion, "We goofed in the early stages." But he insisted that his government had worked hard on the case from the early fifties onward and would continue to do so. Yet only three weeks later the Swedish government again missed an opportunity to press the Soviet on the Wallenberg case. A Soviet submarine ran aground off Sweden's Kariskrona naval base on Oct. 27, precipitating a ten-day diplomatic crisis. Wallenberg activists all over the world urged the Swedes to demand an accounting on Wallenberg before giving up the submarine. The Swedish government tersely replied that the issues were not comparable and finally politely towed the submarine, armed with what were believed to be nuclear warheads, out of Swedish territorial waters.

Swedish timidity notwithstanding, the Wallenberg case can no longer be obscured. It is an international human rights issue and it has even penetrated into the dissident movement within Russia. This means that new facts may come from knowledgeable sources that were never before available.

In March of 1980 the Wallenberg Committee in Stockholm received the following communication from Soviet dissident Andrei Sakharov in exile in Gorki:

For about ten years now I have known about the tragic fate of Raoul Wallenberg. I consider him to be one of those people of the 20th century to whom all of mankind is greatly indebted, and ought to be proud of. I believe the organization of an International Hearing on his case and an international defense campaign on his behalf are very important.

Ever since I learned about him, I have thought a great deal as to possible ways of searching for him. I have spoken with many different kinds of people who at one time or another have passed through Soviet prisons and labor camps, but I have never once succeeded in meeting anyone who could tell me anything about Raoul Wallenberg's fate. Now it seems important to me (although I am not putting too much hope in this) that the Soviet authorities be forced to transfer Raoul Wallenberg's investigation file and his personal prison or labor camp records to the Wallenberg Defense Committee. Since the Soviet authorities have officially admitted that Wallenberg was arrested and was imprisoned in the USSR, then such files must exist (and they are kept forever). It is possible that an investigation file, as well as personal prison or labor camp records will help to shed light on when Raoul Wallenberg was imprisoned and in which prisons or labor camps he was confined. That would make it possible to search for testifiers and eye witnesses precisely from these places of imprisonment.

I realize that it is extremely difficult to obtain any kind of documents from the Soviet authorities, but this should be attempted. At the same time, the refusal of the Soviet authorities to release Wallenberg's files would testify to the fact that they have something to hide. Thus, I believe that the release of Wallenberg's files is the minimal cooperative effort in which the Swedish Government and the Swedish and international community can partake and have every right to demand from the Soviet authorities.

March 21, 1981
Gorky, USSR   */s/ Andrei Sakharov*

EPILOGUE

The fate of Wallenberg became so deeply entangled in the fate of the Hungarian Jews that it would not be fitting to end this history without telling what became of them. Briefly, 501,507 lost their lives in death camps and massacres. Of these 85,453 were from Budapest.

The survivors all suffered loss of loved ones, destruction of homes, property and businesses. The orphans, the widows with young children, those who returned from the camps broken in body and mind, all needed care.

Epidemics and famine struck Budapest with full force after the entrance of the Russian troops. The Jews were restored to instant Hungarian citizenship. That meant they were treated by the Russians like all Hungarians—as enemies—unless they were smart and quick enough to make themselves instantly useful to the Russian authorities. At first, the troops went on an unrestrained looting and raping rampage which left behind thousands of diseased and pregnant women, many of whom committed suicide. Young beautiful women were carried off to camps to be used to death by masses of men. Husbands and fathers lost their lives trying to protect the women.

In his book *It Happened in Budapest,* published in Sweden in 1949, Lars Berg described the conscription of men and women for labor camps in Russia:

A Russian truck came driving up one of the main streets in broad daylight. Suddenly it stopped. A Russian patrol jumped down and surrounded all the people near the truck. The captured people's identification documents were asked for, torn to pieces without being read and thrown into the gutter. With that the newest recruits of the latest five-year plan had been enrolled.

Berg and other observers reported that fierce women soldiers who entered with the Russian troops participated in the pillage and rape, killing men who failed to respond to their sexual demands.

It was many months before the bodies could be pulled out of the rubble of Buda and buried. It was months and years before the remnants of families could be brought together. At first, the Jewish

155

survivors tried to restore their old communities. However, in the wake of the economic devastation of the country, a wave of neo-anti-Semitism rose, and thousands of survivors left Hungary within the next few years. They scattered over the globe, going to Israel, the United States, Canada, Sweden and Australia. Many moved from one country to another, struggling to strike new roots, seeking relatives.

The remaining Jewish community of Budapest did not forget Wallenberg. They were convinced he was dead and wanted to dedicate a memorial to him. They commissioned Pal Patzai, a noted Hungarian sculptor, to design a monument. A friend of Patzai's had been rescued by Wallenberg, and he undertook the assignment with enthusiasm. He designed a heroic bronze figure battling a snake with a swastika head. This rested on a pedestal bearing a relief profile of Wallenberg. The inscription beneath read that the monument was to express "our silent and eternal gratitude to him and should always remind us of his enduring humanity in a period of inhumanity."

The monument was set in its place in St. Stephen's Park, and one Sunday morning in April hundreds of Budapest citizens, community leaders and representatives of the Swedish legation arrived for the dedication. When they reached the appointed spot they found that the eighteen-foot statue and pedestal had been removed during the night!

The statue was found many years later in an abandoned building on the outskirts of Budapest, but the pedestal with the relief portrait of Wallenberg and the inscription was not there. Years later the statue turned up again, set outside a pharmaceutical factory near Debrecen. The swastika had been removed from the serpent's head. The figure in that context appears to be that of Man or Science battling disease. However, many Hungarians are aware that the figure represents Wallenberg.

The Communist regime in Hungary has not attempted to obliterate the name of Wallenberg. He was too great a hero to be forgotten by those who lived through the Nazi occupation, but he has been reduced to insignificance as someone of interest only to Jews. A street in the Jewish neighborhood of Pest has been named for him. The memorial in St. Stephen's Park would have brought him to the constant attention of the general public, including tourists from all over the world.

The Wallenberg case was as submerged in Israel as it was in the rest of the world. The Budapest Jews who came there believed Wallenberg had been killed by the Nazis. They struggled to start new lives and new families in an undeveloped country which had to fight for its existence. They were a small group among hundreds of thousands whose wartime experiences had been just as bad or worse than theirs. Wallenberg was mentioned in personal testimonials in the archives at Yad Vashem, the memorial to the victims of the Holocaust in Jerusalem, and at other Holocaust study centers in Israel, but his role was a mere footnote in a monumental disaster.

Israel came to understand the full Wallenberg story at about the same time as the rest of the world. In 1980 Nina Lagergren and Guy von Dardel traveled there to attend a ceremony in their brother's honor at Yad Vashem. Many Israelis came forward to say that they or members of their family had been saved by Wallenberg. Mrs. Lagergren and Professor von Dardel spoke of their conviction that their brother was still alive in the Gulag.

Russian immigrants in Israel have proven to be an unexpected resource. One of the early Russian immigrants in Israel was Avraham Shifrin, who spent the years from 1953 to 1963 in various Soviet prison camps. His knowledge of the Gulag was so impressive that he was brought to the United States to present testimony on February 1, 1973, to the U.S. Senate Internal Security Subcommittee investigating Soviet labor camps. He said that although thousands of prisoners of war scattered throughout the camps had been repatriated by 1956, he was told shortly before he was released in June 1963 about camps on Wrangell's Island where high-ranking German and Italian officers and other prisoners of war from 1945 were still being held. Shifrin heard the story from prisoners who came from the island. He doubted it at the time, mainly because he knew the island to be a "Godforsaken" frozen waste in the Arctic, about eighty miles north of the mainland of Siberia and a hundred and sixty miles west of Alaska. However, he had recently learned from a new immigrant to Israel who had been on the island in 1962 in a food distributing company that there were in fact many former POW's there.

Shifrin contended that there were thousands of prisoners scattered among three different camps on Wrangell's Island. In one, experiments were being made on live prisoners with radiation, in another there were medical experiments, and in a third, a submarine base, experiments involving human endurance under water.

Shifrin got his information from Efim Moshinsky, a former KGB man who had gotten into trouble and was sentenced to a labor company on Wrangell's Island. Moshinsky was able to remember the names of several prisoners he had seen or heard about. He mentioned the names of Italian officers who were known to be missing. He recalled the name of Alexander Trushnovich, the leader of an anti-Communist group, who had been kidnapped in West Germany, and also of Raoul Wallenberg. The time was the early sixties, some fifteen years after Wallenberg was supposed to have been dead according to the official Soviet version.

An astonishing report about Wallenberg's capture came from a Russian in Israel in the summer of 1981. The man, Yaacov Leontevich Lakhotsky-Menaker, claimed that he had done research in military history in Russia and interviewed officers of units which entered Budapest in 1945. One told of having participated in a very important political operation—the capture of a Swedish diplomat Raoul Wallenberg who had contacts with the Gestapo. Menaker pointed out that Brezhnev was at that time chief of the political section of the 18th Army, which entered Hungary via Rumania. Menaker reasoned that therefore Brezhnev had been personally responsible for ordering Wallenberg's arrest. Menaker's story created a media furor in Sweden in August 1981, but it led to no new trails in the search for Wallenberg. There has been no confirmation or denial of this story from any official source.

Many other reports of contacts with Wallenberg, both direct and indirect, have come to the attention of the Wallenberg Committee and the Swedish Foreign Office over the years. The reports were remarkably consistent, varied sources confirming each other with telling details (see appendix). The testimony that most strongly impressed Simon Wiesenthal with the fact that Wallenberg was alive in the Soviet Union after 1947 was that of Dr. Menachem Meltzer, an Austrian Jew who had studied medicine in the Soviet Union and worked as a doctor in the northern Urals. Meltzer told of having examined a Swede named Raoul in the summer of 1948 in a camp called Khal'mer Yu. He noted that the Swede had a strong heart. Meltzer was presented with a large group of portrait photos and picked out a photo of Wallenberg as the Swede he had examined.

A more indirect report came from a Dane, Mogens Carlson, who said that in February 1951 in Butyrka prison he met Zoltan Rivo, a

Hungarian professor of languages, who said that for about a week at New Year's time he had shared his cell with a Swedish diplomat. Two Germans, H.T. Mulle and C. Rehekampf, reported that in 1956 in Vladimir prison they shared a cell with a Georgian writer named Gogoveritse, who had been there since 1945, and who named Wallenberg as a prisoner who was kept isolated in a special wing of the building.

Reports of Wallenberg's being in Vladimir in the fifties were further confirmed by Emile Brügger, a Swiss, who said he had had knocking contact there in 1954 with a prisoner who identified himself as Wallenberg. The prisoner asked Brugger if he were released to report to some Swedish consulate that he was not permitted to write or receive letters. An Austrian, who did not wish to have his name revealed, also reported a contact with Wallenberg in the prison hospital at Vladimir. He said that the prisoner gave his name as Wallenberg and told him that if he forgot the name when he was set free he should say he had encountered a "a Swede from Budapest."

In contrast to the startlingly consistent and poignant quality of the statements from returned prisoners from the Gulag, the reports of his death range from a too-easy acceptance of the Russian version of the matter to bizarre theories. Among those who promoted the concept that Wallenberg had died at the hands of Nazis or brigands outside of Budapest were the Hungarian journalist-historian Lévai and a Russian interpreter at the Swedish Legation, Count Kutuzov-Tolstoy. Kutuzov-Tolstoy managed to get himself employed by the Russians soon after they entered Budapest and continued to work for them for many years after. Levai, who had detailed Wallenberg's heroism in an earlier book, as a writer living in Soviet-dominated Hungary, came to tailor his writing to the regime, and by 1961 when he published his book *Eichmann in Hungary* left Wallenberg out completely.

The most imaginative of several tales of Wallenberg's death was that of a Swedish woman, Britt Ehrenstrale, who reported that she knew that Wallenberg had died as the result of injuries suffered when Polish partisans blew up a Soviet prison train in 1945. She had encountered a dying man, his face covered with bandages. When the partisans told her he was Swedish, she asked him to press her hand if his name was Raoul Wallenberg. She believed she felt a light hand pressure in response.

In December 1981, the Swedish press reported that a writer working on a book on Wallenberg received positive information from former Prime Minister Erlander and Professor Svartz that they had known since 1965 that Wallenberg died in prison that year. Both Svartz and Erlander denied vociferously that they had ever received information about Wallenberg's death other than the official statements or that they had given such information to the writer.

Another death report came in 1981 at a meeting between Ronald Greenwald, an American rabbi, and Wolfgang Vogel, an East Berlin lawyer with contacts in Soviet political circles. The two had met many times to arrange spy and prisoner swaps between the Soviet Union and Western countries. Greenwald, at the request of Mrs. Lagergren and Professor von Dardel, brought a picture of Wallenberg and asked about him. Vogel immediately responded that Wallenberg had been dead a long time. However, Greenwald told this writer in an interview in New York, January 22, 1982, that although he has a great deal of trust in Vogel, he is aware that "if the Russians wanted me to believe he's dead that's what they would say." The fact that Vogel has been effectively representing the Soviets in the prisoner exchanges indicates that he is speaking for the same official sources that have always insisted upon Wallenberg's death.

In the fall of 1980 I visited Budapest in search of a feeling of reality about the events of 1944 and 1945. It was a shock to see a clean, beautiful city bustling with tourist activity. Budapest is the showplace capital of East Europe. It has beautifully manicured parks and recreational centers, newly reconstructed medieval buildings, excellent public transportation. Tantalizing odors waft out of the food shops and restaurants. In the opulent old-world atmosphere of the café at Vöröszmarty Square, the building from which the Arrow Cross band had dragged out Tom Veres's parents, young tourists in jeans mingle with elegantly dressed elderly ladies and gentlemen sipping coffee and devouring delectable pastries. Few tourists note the shell scars and bullet holes on the buildings. Most of these marks are souvenirs of the 1956 uprising.

I managed to meet a relative of Langfelder's, who spoke glowingly of Wallenberg, but looked at me with some amusement ("a daffy American!") when I mentioned the possibility of Wallenberg's being alive. He appeared to have no knowledge that both Wallenberg and Langfelder were reported to have been seen in prison in Moscow in February 1945. There are no further reports about sightings of Langfelder after that date. Even if Langfelder lived for many years after, it was highly unlikely that any report would come back about him. There were thousands of Hungarian prisoners in Russia, but Wallenberg was the only Swedish diplomat, and probably the only Swede, imprisoned from the 1950s on. Most of the reports that came back about Wallenberg had some distinguishing identification information—such as "a Swede from Budapest," "prominent family," "Swedish diplomat." Langfelder was one of multitudes.

A Budapest lawyer who had served on Wallenberg's staff spoke enthusiastically about him. He recalled his dedication, intensity and capacity for work, and noted that he inspired others to live up to his standards. "When he told you to do something, you knew it had to get done." When I asked whether he had been present on the occasion of the dedication of the memorial that disappeared, he made a gesture indicating the walls had ears and offered to walk me to my bus stop. As we walked slowly in the street, he informed me that he had been present at that strange event, but had nothing further to say about it. When I told him about the reports that Wallenberg was still alive, he shook his head incredulously. Finally he said, "Forget it. Go home. There was no Wallenberg. There were no Jews, no Holocaust. Our children don't want to hear about it. We are all trying to live today."

My informant was only partially correct. Many young Hungarian Jews are assimilating into the general population, but others are trying to hold on to their history, traditions and identity. There is no discrimination against Jews in the government, the professions or the arts. Dr. Laszlo Salgo, the chief rabbi of Hungary, president of the Budapest Rabbinical Council and rabbi of the Dohany Street Synagogue, was elected a member of Parliament from the 17th Electoral District in June 1980. The government partially subsidizes religious institutions. A kosher kitchen serves meals to elderly pensioners, and each year a matzo factory produces tons of matzoth, some of which are shipped to Poland, Czechoslovakia and East Germany.

Budapest has the only remaining rabbinical seminary in East Europe. At one time there were thousands studying there. When I visited there were seventeen rabbinical students, including some from Czechoslovakia, Bulgaria and even the Soviet Union. The rector is Dr. Sandor Scheiber, a specialist in manuscript study and a world-renowned scholar of Jewish folklore and comparative literature. He is a charismatic figure to the young people who flock to his informal Friday evening talks and *oneg Shabbat* (Sabbath celebration).

In my three separate, long meetings with him, Dr. Scheiber talked with evident pain about the loss of seven hundred congregations in the richly varied Jewish communities of his country, and each time spoke about the loss of his mother on New Year's Eve 1944, when the Arrow Cross band broke into the Glass House and threw their grenades. A plaque at the front door of the school notes that it was the first Nazi collecting station in the city, and that twenty thousand went to their deaths from this place.

The Dohany Street Synagogue, built in 1854 to seat three thousand, is a magnificent Byzantine and Moorish-style building which fills to overflowing on high holidays. Attached to it is the Jewish Museum, containing relics from the old synagogues and an exhibition devoted to the Holocaust. The synagogue's garden contains 2,380 graves of those killed in Budapest. There is a special memorial to Hannah Szenes, whose body was brought to Israel. There are memorial plaques for those whose bodies were lost in the fires of Auschwitz and in the waters of the Danube. And there is a plaque outside the building commemorating the day the Red Army liberated that area of the city—the day Wallenberg vanished.

On a bright, early fall day I stood on top of Castle Hill, where Raoul Wallenberg stood with Tom Veres on January 6, 1945, watching the Russians tighten their hold around the city. Sunshine glistened from the rooftops, and small white cloud puffs skittered across a bright blue sky. Traffic flowed across the rebuilt bridges of the Danube. The river sparkled along its sinuous length, bisecting the city. To the north the gentle hills drift off into dreamy distance. Among them is Rose Hill, where Eichmann lived in voluptuous luxury while he concocted new diabolical schemes. To the south is Gellért Hill, rising 770 feet and topped by a 110-foot heroic statue, the Liberation Monument, dedicated to the Russian soldiers who died taking the city from the Germans.

Tourists flock to the top of both hills to enjoy one of the most beguiling views in Europe. Perhaps a few of them think about the great battle that was fought there and the lives that were lost. Very few of them know about the man who once stood there, hoping the Russians would come soon.

Raoul Wallenberg would love the view of the city today. He was not built for sainthood or martyrdom. He loved the outdoors, beautiful buildings, a well-planned city, commercial enterprise, the company of civilized humans. He was a practical man who cared about decency. His soul was forged in two centuries of enlightenment, in the ideals of humanism, fraternity and progress. It was his passion for those values that trapped him into the new age of darkness.

Is Raoul Wallenberg alive today? It is possible. He comes of a hardy, long-lived breed, and he brought with him into prison rich psychological resources. Perhaps yet today something in the quality of the man speaks to even the most hardened of prison guards. Perhaps some feel pity for him in his age and long incarceration. Perhaps he has found a *modus vivendi* in the prison environment in these long years, being a man of imagination and a believer in life.

Will Raoul Wallenberg ever return? It is not impossible. Sovietologists agree that little is predictable about the Soviet Union. A new regime brought about by new leadership or other factors could produce an upheaval or significant policy changes. As long as the West keeps up its interest in the case, there is always the chance that errors may be admitted and long-buried secrets unearthed. And as long as the file containing the truth about Raoul Wallenberg exists deep in the prison archives of the Soviet Union, there is the possibility that the full story will emerge.

APPENDIX

In 1957 the Royal Swedish Foreign Office published a set of documents concerning the Raoul Wallenberg case up to that date. It included testimony from eighteen returned prisoners from the Soviet Union who reported direct contacts with Wallenberg or his driver, Vilmos Langfelder, in Lubianka Prison and later Lefortovo, both in Moscow. The testimonies were given under oath and were taken under special conditions set by the chief of the investigation, Otto Danielsson. Hearsay was excluded and witnesses were not informed about the testimony of others.

Communication in prison was reported as extremely difficult. The following is an excerpt from the Swedish documents describing the conditions and explaining prison telegraphy:

The Lefortovskaja Prison consists of a brick building formed like a K with four floors. The main part of the building lies in connection with a large walled courtyard. The other buildings around this courtyard have three floors and in these the court and examination premises are to be found. A wing containing the administrative department of the prison together with certain residential premises lies in connection with the side of the prison that faces the street.

The Lefortovskaja Prison is of a so-called gallery type. The cells face a 5 m broad shaft going straight across the four floors. A person, standing at a point A can from there watch all the cell doors. Outside the cells there is a kind of bridge, about 70–80 cm wide. A strong wire-netting forms a protection from the shaft. On each floor are four guards, one for each wing, together with an inspector. At the point A the so-called "flag-man" had his place. When a prisoner had to be moved from or to his cell, the guard in question first had to get a sign from the flag-man before the moving. Because of this system the prisoners never got a chance of seeing other prisoners than their cell companions.

The floors are connected with each other by three staircases. Moreover there is a provision-lift. On the ground floor of a special little building, added to and connected with the main part, one finds a barber, photographer and library. On the second floor are the pharma-

cists and the surgeries of a doctor and a dentist. The baths are in the basement. The Lefortovskaja Prison can house a little more than 600 prisoners. Mostly, however, the average number was smaller. Usually three prisoners were put in the same cell.

A door plated on each side leads to the cell. On the door there is a peephole at the height for the eyes, and a kind of a window which closes from the outside and through which the food is brought. Every two or three minutes the guard peeped through the hole to see what was going on in the cell. The size of the cells is 3 x 2.4 m. To the right or left of the door is a toilet and a washstand with running water. One bed is placed on each longside of the room and one at the window. The window has bars and also a special boxlike shelter which only lets the light in from above. In the middle of the room is a small table. All the walls are thick. The ceiling is vaulted.

The daily routine included a 20 minutes' walk in one of the eight sections of the courtyard. These are 5 x 3.5 m big and surrounded by a wall about 3 m high. Up to 1945 these special sections were placed in the triangle-shaped yard, formed by the wings of the building's built-in angle. After that the sections were placed in the big courtyard.

In the library the prisoners could borrow books in Russian. Papers were forbidden, nor were the prisoners allowed to possess writing material. Once in two weeks a prisoner could ask for paper, pen and ink if he wanted to present a wish or a demand to the administration.

In spite of the severe regulations in the prison concerning everything that could be used as a way to communication, there were certain possibilities to get information. At first hand the interest was drawn to those who shared the same fate quite nearby. The most important method of communication was the so-called prison telegraphy. It could be used through different systems. The most common was the so-called "idiot system," that is one knock = A, two = b, three = c, etc. One form of this system was the "five-by-five system," usually called the square system. To knock through this system was to knock a certain number of times to mark the row and then a number of times to mark the column for each letter. (For L: first three knocks and, after a short break, two knocks.) [See page 166.]

Only very seldom the Morse alphabet was used.

The knockings were of course forbidden, and they had to be most careful. A toothbrush was a good knocking tool. To hide the knocking a prisoner could sit on his bed with his back against the wall

	1	2	3	4	5
1	A	B	C	D	E
2	F	G	H	I	J
3	K	L	M	N	O
4	P	Q	R	S	T
5	U	V	X	Y	Z

and a book on his lap. The hand farthest away from the cell door did the knocking. The arm was not in the sleeve, which was arranged as if it were. The guard looking through the peephole could thus see nothing suspicious. The brick walls and the vaulted ceilings in the cells of the Lefortovskaja Prison are most appropriate for prison telegraphy. The wall to the outside is about 60 cm thick, the wall between the cells about 25–30 cm and the wall to the shaft about 45–50 cm.

Another way of communication was through the water pipes. On the top floor these were often empty, especially in summer, because of insufficient water pressure. If the taps were then opened the prisoners could talk with the one of the neighboring cells which had its water pipes in common with the first mentioned. On the whole the water pipes conducted the sounds very well. With help of a funnel-shaped thing, put against the pipe, a prisoner could "telephone" with the prisoners in the neighboring cell. In the bath, every ten days, the prisoners took their chance of calling their names to each other, and sometimes it was also possible to exchange some words there.

The knocking information usually contained news from the prison; for example, if somebody had been brought to examination. If a new prisoner arrived, one wanted to know his name, where he had been arrested and for what reason, etc. The prisoners also exchanged addresses, so that the one that first returned home could inform the relatives.

It sometimes happened that so-called cell spies were put in the cells. In order to avoid the latter's provoking knocking information the prisoners mostly used special calling and receiving signs for the different cells. If it was possible for the prisoners to stay for a rather long *time in the same part of the prison, they could reach far with help of the prison telegraph when they wanted to know who was in the neighborhood. If the prisoners knew each other from before or at least had heard of each other, the communications between the cells were of course made easier. By chance, both these factors were present in the part of the Lefortovskaja Prison, where R.W. was placed in the spring of 1945.*

As the Russian troops at the offensive in Europe advanced, the prisoners at first were brought to temporary camps. Certain important categories of prisoners—e.g., high officers and legation staff—after one or two weeks were sent by special transport, mostly by air, to Moscow. In Moscow mainly three prisons were used: Lefortovskaja, Butyrkja and Ljubljanskaja. Part of the German and Italian legation staff was brought to Lefortovskaja Prison and was there put on the second floor. During the first half of the year 1945 thus representatives from Bucharest (B) and Sofia (S) were put in the cells 149–153 on the second floor.

The following are excerpts from reports of released prisoners. Wallenberg is referred to as R.W. Certain minor discrepancies appear in the various reports. However, these may be attributed to lapses in comprehension or in memory. The testimony was taken about ten years after the events described.

Gustav Richter—Former police attaché at the German legation in Bucharest. He was arrested in August 1944 and flown to Moscow, where he was put first in Lefortovo and then moved to Lubianka:

On the 31st January 1945 Raoul Wallenberg, secretary at the Swedish legation in Budapest, was put into the cell.

R.W. and I soon became friends. During the month we spent together in the Ljubljanskaja Prison he kept his spirits up and was in a good mood. R.W. told me that he had been sent to Budapest to help the Hungarian Jews by giving them Swedish protection passports. He had had great difficulties with the German authorities (representatives for the secret state police) in Budapest. As soon as the Russian troops had reached the city, R.W. had reported himself to the Russian military authorities. They had sent him from one department to another, together with his driver, Langfelder, and finally they had been arrested. They were both brought by train via Rumania to Moscow, where they were put into the Ljubljanskaja Prison. At the arrival at the prison R.W. and Langfelder were separated.

R.W. did not talk much about his relatives but he mentioned his mother and aunt. He said several times, "What will my relatives say when they learn that I am imprisoned?" He was very particular about his reputation. I comforted him by saying that under those circumstances that would be no shame.

R.W. also told me that he belonged to a well-known banker's family in Sweden and had studied architecture in America and that his profession was architect. R.W. spoke perfect English and German. During the time we shared the cell we changed addresses, and I still remember quite clearly that I got from him a piece of paper with his name written down by hand, on which the Foreign Office in Stockholm was stated as his address. This piece of paper was taken away from me at an inspection.

Some time at the beginning of February 1945 R.W. wrote a letter addressed to the director of the prison, in which he protested against the treatment and against his becoming arrested. R.W. also referred to his Swedish citizenship and his status as diplomat and demanded the right to get in touch with the Swedish legation in Moscow. R.W. handed over this letter to the guard (Starji) on duty on the ground floor.

During the time R.W. spent together with me in the Ljubljanskaja Prison, he was only questioned one time. The inspector leading the examination among other things said to him: "Well, you are well known to us. You belong to a great capitalist family in Sweden." R.W. was accused of espionage. The examination lasted about 1–1½ hours.

Karl Suprian—Former secretary general at the German Scientific Institute in Bucharest, attached to the German legation. He was arrested August 23, 1944, in Bucharest and imprisoned there and in Greece before being brought to Moscow by air. He was in Lefortovo between September 1944 and October 1948. He communicated via knocking with adjoining cells and one on the fourth floor of the prison:

To 1947 I had continuous contact through knocking with the "Councillor of legation of the 1st class" in Bucharest, Mr. Willi Roedel, well known to me from Bucharest, and with his cell companion R.W., secretary at the Swedish legation in Budapest. Usually I knocked directly to Roedel, but in some cases also to R.W.

Roedel informed me about R.W., that he belonged to a well-known Swedish family, and that he had been the head of an action to help the Jews in Budapest. R.W. was accused by the Russians for

*espionage, but sat "since a year and a day without examination." When
I was first informed of the presence of a Swedish diplomat in the prison I
was so surprised that I asked Roedel once more to confirm his report to
avoid misunderstanding. Roedel repeated his information. Later I many
times asked, "What does the Swede do?" or "Is the Swede still there?"
which Roedel each time clearly answered to.*

    Claudio de Mohr—Former Italian consul in Bulgaria. Taken
prisoner by Soviet troops at the border between Bulgaria and Turkey, he
was brought to Debrecen and from there to Moscow by air. He
remained in Cell 152 in Lefortovo Prison from September 1944 to April
1948. At the end of April 1945 he and his cell mates heard two new
prisoners being brought to Cell 151:

*At first we did not contact them. Very early one morning I heard our
neighbors in Cell 151 communicating a long time by knockings with
another cell. We grasped later half of the report, and we could
understand that one of the prisoners in German related that he had
been arrested by the Russians in Budapest in January 1945. Then we
tried to get direct connection with the prisoners in 151 and in this way
we learnt that one of our neighbors was the German councillor of
legation Willy Roedel and the other Mr. R.W. from the Swedish legation
in Budapest. We were so surprised that a Swedish diplomat had been
arrested that we many times asked for confirmation, which was given to
us.*

    Ernst Wallenstein—Former scientific assistant at the German
legation in Bucharest, he was arrested there on September 2, 1944, and
brought by air to Moscow and placed in Lefortovo Prison. He and his
cell mates established knocking connections with some of their
neighbors:

*Our contact with R.W. and Roedel started about the change of year
1945–46. I still remember quite clearly the time for this, as R.W. had the
intention to write a letter of protest and was not quite sure to whom he
ought to send it. Through knockings we agreed that it would be best to
send it to Stalin himself and that it should be written in French. I
suggested to address Stalin as* "Monsieur le Président," *and also
suggested the polite phrase* "Agréez, Monsieur le Président, l'expression
de ma trés haute consideration." *I know that R.W. wrote such a letter and
had it sent away by the guard.*

Bernard Rensinghoff—Former commercial adviser at the German legation in Bucharest, he was arrested there September 2, 1944, brought by air to Moscow and placed in Lefortovo. He and his cell mates used the "idiot system" to establish knocking connections with neighboring cells:

In a cell on the third floor, straight above us, were the German citizens Styhler, Rösstel and Bergemann. Beside these sat Roedel, a councillor at the German legacy in Bucharest, and the Swedish diplomat R.W.. The contact between me and the two in the cell above became most intensive. Every day we exchanged messages. Roedel as well as R.W. were eager knockers. In this way R.W. told me about his activity in Budapest and about his being arrested. As his address R.W. stated Stockholm. Our cell companion Josias von Rantzau told us about the Wallenbergs, whom he knew of from his time in Stockholm.

During the first period our knocking connections were mostly used to compose a letter in French. In this letter R.W. referred to his diplomatic status and asked to be examined. R.W. had sent this letter to Stalin in the summer of 1946 with a request to get a chance of contacting the Swedish legacy in Moscow. Concerning the choice of French words he asked among others Rantzau for advice. After some time R.W. got a message, in which the despatch of his letter was confirmed.

Soon before the removal of R.W. and Roedel, R.W. was brought to an examination. After the questioning R.W. himself knocked a message similar to this: The inspector had informed him that his case was quite clear, and that he was a "political case." If he considered himself innocent, it was his responsibility to prove this. The best proof of his guilt was the fact that the Swedish legacy in Moscow and the Swedish government had done nothing on his case. R.W. had asked the inspector, who held the examination, to be allowed to contact directly the Swedish legacy in Moscow or with the Red Cross or at least to write to them. This request was refused with "Nobody cares about you. If the Swedish government or its legation had taken any interest in you, they would long ago have contacted you."

On another occasion R.W. informed us that he had asked an officer if he would be sentenced or not. He got the answer: "For political reasons you will never be sentenced."

With the exception of the formal examination at his entrance into the prison, this was R.W.'s first examination.

Except for this message, only one more short message came: "We are being taken away," together with some blows of the fists, probably when they were taken out. This happened during 1946, as far as I can remember in the fall.

Erhard Hille—former corporal in the German Wehrmacht, he was arrested in Kurland, January 12, 1945, brought to Moscow on March 6, 1945, and first placed in Lubianka and then in Lefortovo:

On March 22, 1945, the Hungarian citizen Vilmos Langfelder from Budapest was brought into the cell. Langfelder had red-blond hair, a round face and was about 170 cm tall. He was born in 1912 or 1913 and was a Jew. Langfelder was an engineer. His family owned a machine factory in Budapest, which during the war was taken over by the Göring concern (Reichswerke Hermann Göring). The greatest stockholder was his grandmother, who was then still alive. However, Langfelder did not work in the family business, but worked as consulting engineer and designer until the Nazis took power.

In September–October 1944 Langfelder took the job as driver of the secretary at the Swedish legation in Budapest. About his experiences he related as follows:

After Budapest had been surrounded by the Russian troops, R.W., accompanied by L. in the beginning of January 1945, tried to get into contact with the Russian headquarters to try to prevent further bombardment at the legation block, as there were no bulletproof shelters there. The departments with which R.W. got connection declared that they could not give such orders, and advised him to turn directly to Marshal Malinovsky. However, R.W. and L. after that were arrested by a NKVD major. This happened three or four days after R.W. had contacted the Russian staff.

Later R.W. and L. were taken via Rumania to Moscow, where they—as far as I can remember—on the 6th February 1945 were brought into the Ljubljanskaja Prison. There they were separated from each other. After that Langfelder had not seen R.W.

Langfelder was brought into a cell, in which he up to the 18th March 1945 sat together with Mr. Roedel, councillor at the German legation in Bucharest and a Czech. During his stay in the Ljubljanskaja Prison, Langfelder was questioned twice about the conditions concerning his being arrested.

On the 18th March Langfelder was brought from the Ljubljanskaja Prison to the Lefortovskaja Prison, where he was sitting alone for the first three days. After that he came to Cell 105, where I was sitting since the 6th March 1945. Langfelder and I sat together to the 6th April 1945, when I was brought over to the Butyrskaja Prison, Cell 287. Since then I have not seen Langfelder again. During the following years, however, I met other prisoners who had been Langfelder's cell companions.

During the following months I sat in different cells. Among my cell companions from this time was Hans Loyda, born in Czechoslovakia in 1912, but when about twenty became a German citizen, as his parents then moved to Germany.

During a conversation with Loyda in November 1946 I asked him if he had been sitting together with Langfelder in the Ljubljanskaja Prison. Loyda answered yes and said that he was "the Czech." Then Loyda told me as follows: After Langfelder was brought away on the 18th March 1945 R.W. came to the cell in his place.

R.W. was a very good companion and asked the Russian officer to give his cigarettes to Langfelder. During the time R.W. sat together with Loyda, he was brought to examination several times. R.W. had said that the Russians did not have any reason to keep him imprisoned at all. He had worked for the Russians in Budapest. This the Russians did not believe. The leaders of the examinations said that R.W. was a rich Swedish capitalist, and what would such a man do for the Russians. In the middle of May 1945 all three were brought away from the Ljubljanskaja Prison in a prisoners' carriage. Through an opening in the carriage Loyda saw that R.W. and Roedel were brought out at the Lefortovskaja Prison. Loyda was then himself brought to the Butyrskaja Prison.

The foreign office documents list four cell mates of R.W.'s in Lubianka and Lefortovo, and eight who sat with Langfelder. Of these only Richter, Huber, Hille and Horst Kitschmann (one of Langfelder's cell mates) returned from Russian captivity up to the time of the report.

Additional testimony showed that Richter, Huber and Kitschmann were all called for special interrogation about R.W. and L.

late in July or early in August 1947. Hille was at that time in another prison in Kransogorsk.

Richter gave the following testimony:

On the 27th July 1947 at about ten in the evening I was brought to an examination in the Lefortovskaja Prison. The questioning was led by a colonel from the Office for Home Affairs (NKVD). Beside him stood an interpreter, a lieutenant-colonel, who talked good German. I was asked with which persons I had been sharing cells during my imprisonment.

I said the names and thereby also the name Wallenberg. They then asked me for whom I had related about R.W. I answered that I had told my cell companions Wilhelm Rodde and Franz Langer about R.W. I also had to relate what R.W. had told me. I also told Admiral Werner Tillessen, who entered the cell after Franz Langer moved out, about the R.W. case.

After the examination I was brought to another cell, where I spent two weeks alone without permission to go out at all. After that I was placed in Cell 72 and then, because of repairs in the prison, in Cell 79. Up to the 23rd February I had to remain alone in these cells.

Testimony from Ernst Huber and Horst Kitschmann follows a similar pattern. Erhard Hille, who was in Kransogorsk, later learned from another former cell mate of Langfelder's that he and a third cell mate had been subjected to the interrogation and subsequent isolation.

The foreign office concludes as follows:

The reason for these examinations seems chiefly to be an attempt to learn how much these prisoners knew about L. and R.W. After the hearings it must have been clear to the leader of the examinations that the prisoners questioned knew a great deal about R.W's activity in Budapest and about his and Langfelder's experiences after they were arrested. The treatment the questioned prisoners got after the examinations shows that the Russian authorities wished as far as possible to prevent the information about the Swedish diplomat from spreading.

NOTES ON SOURCES

The Wallenberg story cannot be understood fully and accurately unless it is placed against the background of the events that led up to it, those that occurred simultaneously with Wallenberg's mission and those that occurred immediately after he left Budapest. In painting this vast landscape, I selected details that served to illuminate the general political-military situation, Sweden's role as a neutral and the situation of the Jews, targeted for destruction before the war began.

In addition to the bibliography listed below, my sources for this book include personal interviews and correspondence with men and women who knew Raoul Wallenberg at various phases of his life, and a few who saw him only once, at some critical moment in Budapest. The names of the individuals and the circumstances of their encounters with Wallenberg are given in the text. I also used testimonies from the archives at Yad Vashem Martyrs' and Heroes' Remembrance Authority and the Central Zionist Archives in Jerusalem; the YIVO Institute for Jewish Research, New York; the United States War Refugee Board file (Box 111) in the Franklin D. Roosevelt Memorial Library at Hyde Park; and the U.S. State Department, Unclassified Documents on Wallenberg. I consulted the archives of the American Jewish Joint Distribution Committee.

For material directly pertaining to Wallenberg I used the following:

Anger, Per. *With Raoul Wallenberg in Budapest*. New York: Holocaust Library, 1981.

Berg, Lars. *It Happened in Budapest*. Stockholm: 1949.

Bierman, John. *Righteous Gentile*. New York: Viking, 1981.

174

von Dardel, Fredrik. *Raoul Wallenberg*. Stockholm: Proprius Förlag, 1970.

Derogy, Jacques. *Le Cas Wallenberg*. Paris: Editions Ramsay, 1980.

Lévai, Jenö. *Raoul Wallenberg: His Fascinating Life, His Daring Struggles, and the Secret of His Mysterious Disappearance*. Budapest: Magyar Téka, 1948.

Philipp, Rudolph. *Raoul Wallenberg: Diplomat, Kämpe, Samarit*. Stockholm: Fredborgs Forlag, 1946; rev. ed. Stockholm, 1980.

Sjöquist, Eric. *The Raoul Wallenberg Affair*. Stockholm: Bonniers, 1974.

Swedish Foreign Office Documents. *Raoul Wallenberg*. Released in White Books 1957, 1965, 1980.

For material on the Holocaust in Hungary, the Holocaust in general and the political and military situation in Hungary I used the following:

Bauer, Yehuda. "The Mission of Joel Brand," in *The Holocaust in Perspective*. Seattle: The University of Washington Press, 1978.

Biss, André. *A Million Jews to Save*. Cranbury, N.J.: A.S. Barnes & Co., 1975.

Braham, Randolph L. *The Politics of Genocide: The Holocaust in Hungary*, 2 vols. New York: Columbia University Press, 1981.

Braham, Randolph L., ed. *Hungarian-Jewish Studies*, 3 vols. New York: World Federation of Hungarian Jews, 1973.

Fenyo, Mario. *Hitler, Horthy and Hungary*. New Haven: Yale University Press. 1972.

Hausner, Gideon. *Justice in Jerusalem*. New York: Harper & Row, 1966.

Heyman, Éva. *The Diary of Éva Heyman*. Jerusalem: Yad Vashem, 1974.

Hilberg, Raul. *The Destruction of the European Jews*. Chicago: Quadrangle, 1967.

Horthy, Miklós. *Memoirs*. New York: R. Speller, 1957.

Lévai, Jenö. *Black Book on the Martyrdom of Hungarian Jewry*. Vienna: The Central European Times Publishing Co. Ltd., Zurich, in conjunction with the Panorama Publishing Co. Ltd., 1948.

————. *Eichmann in Hungary.* Budapest: Pannonia Press, 1961.

Lukacs, John. *1945 Year Zero.* New York: Doubleday, 1978.

Macartney, C.A. *October Fifteenth.* Edinburgh: University of Edinburgh, 1961.

Reitlinger, Gerald. *The Final Solution: The Attempt to Exterminate the Jews of Europe 1939–1945,* 2nd rev. and enlarged ed. South Brunswick, N.J.: Yoseloff, 1961.

Weissberg, Alex. *Desperate Mission: Joel Brand's Story as told to Alex Weissberg,* trans. Constantine Fitzgibbon and Andrew Foster-Melliar. New York: Criterion, 1958.

Wiesel, Elie. *Night, Dawn, The Accident: Three Tales.* New York: Hill and Wang, 1972.

The moral and political implications of Wallenberg's mission must be viewed as part of the totality of the Holocaust and of the general failure of the world to grasp the facts and respond appropriately to the Nazi program of genocide. I found valuable background in the following:

Feingold, Henry L. *The Politics of Rescue: The Roosevelt Administration and the Holocaust, 1938–1945.* New Brunswick, N.J.: Rutgers University Press, 1970.

Gilbert, Martin. *Auschwitz and the Allies.* New York: Holt, Rinehart and Winston, 1981.

Laqueur, Walter. *The Terrible Secret.* Boston, Toronto: Little Brown and Company, 1980.

Marrus, Michael R. and Paxton, Robert O. *Vichy France and the Jews.* New York: Basic Books, 1981.

Morse, Arthur D. *While Six Million Died: A Chronicle of American Apathy.* New York: Random House, 1968.

Wyman, David. "Why Auschwitz Was Never Bombed." *Commentary* 65, No. 5 (May 1978).

Wallenberg's story is a significant part of Swedish history in World War II and part of the history of the Cold War. I found the best resources in the following books:

Carlgren, W.M. *Swedish Foreign Policy During the Second World War.* London & Tornbridge: Ernest Benn Ltd., 1977.

Feis, Herbert. *Churchill, Roosevelt and Stalin: The War They Waged and the Peace They Sought,* (2nd ed.). Princeton: Princeton University Press, 1967.

Foreign Relations of the United States, 1944, Europe, Vol. IV. U.S. Government Printing Office, 1966.

Kennan, George F. *Memoirs, 1925–1950.* Boston, Toronto: Little, Brown and Company, 1967.

Lundestad, Geir. *America, Scandinavia and the Cold War.* New York: Columbia University Press, 1980.

Mastny, Vojtech. *Russia's Road to the Cold War.* New York: Columbia University Press, 1979.

INDEX